Don't Bite Me, I'm Santa Claus

Tom Plummer

SHADOW MOUNTAIN.

To Bill and Christine Bracy:
the best Santa act around.

Library of Congress Cataloging-in-Publication Data

Plummer, Tom, 1939–
    Don't bite me, I'm Santa Claus / Tom Plummer.
      p.   cm.
    ISBN 1-57345-538-5
    1. Santa Claus.   2. Christmas.   I. Title.
GT4992.P58   1999
394.2663—dc21
                                          99-35285
                                            CIP

Printed in the United States of America   18961-6478

10 9 8 7 6 5 4 3 2 1

Contents

Introduction

A Gift for Santa

by Louise Plummer

It is almost impossible to surprise Santa Claus with a gift. He's used to giving, but not receiving. The Santa Claus at our house knows who's been naughty and nice, and he also knows what's inside every box, including the ones intended for him. I'll call him Tom, since to call him any derivation of "saint" on a day-to-day basis starts up my gag reflex. Tom has been known to say, while holding a gift up to his ear and shaking it like a cantaloupe, "Oh, this must be a tie wrapped in a Crisco can," or, "This must be a camera bag," or, "Two videos and a book." Even more irritating is when he guesses what he's getting before it's been wrapped, before it even enters the house.

So over the years it has become my aim to surprise Tom with a gift. No easy feat.

One year my student Amy Jorgensen, who was an art major, showed me a series of black-and-white photographs she had done for a final project. Each photograph was neatly matted. As she carefully placed them in front of me one by one, I admired her talent for seeing the artistry in the grill of an old truck or a barbed wire fence or a broken pot. "I wish Tom could see these," I said. "Maybe it would inspire him back to photography. How did you do these?"

"I used a pinhole camera," Amy said.

I thought she was joking. "You mean like the kind the Boy Scouts make out of milk cartons?"

"Yes. I used a fancier one, but the principle is the same." She brought out a beautiful box camera made of a polished wood. "This one is handmade by a guy in Colorado."

"Tom would love this," I said, stroking the camera.

"I'll get you the phone number," she said. "It takes about six weeks for delivery. He only makes them as the orders come in."

With the phone number in my pocket, I sang "Santa, Baby" all the way home, sounding remarkably like Eartha Kitt. I called the camera maker in Colorado Springs and gave him my credit-card number. He assured me that the camera would be there before Christmas.

Then I made my big mistake: I got all feminine. Sounding like one of the three little maids from school, I danced around Tom and said, "I've bought you the most wonderful Christmas present, and you'll never guess what it is. Oh, I'm so excited. I'm out-of-my-mind excited."

He liked this game. "Give me a hint."

"Oh, no, no—I know what you'll do. You'll guess it. No hints. Absolutely none. You'll never guess. You'll never guess." It came out like a little song made up in a dark corner of an insane asylum.

Three days later, he said, "You're giving me a pinhole camera."

Give me a break.

This knocked the wind out of my look-for-a-surprise-for-Tom ambitions for several years. He received a cashmere overcoat, an Irish hand-knit sweater, and other tasteful but uninspired gifts. He liked these offerings, but I never cared if he guessed or not, and because I didn't care, he didn't try. There was no holiday tension in this kind of giving and getting. It was boring.

But then came the year we—my sons and I—gave him an African Gray parrot. It was a perfect present for Tom, who had dreamed of owning one ever since he had read an article in *Harper's* magazine by an African Gray owner. That parrot sang arias. Tom wanted a singing parrot. Then, too, our friends Ken and Ann bought a parrot, and it would sit on Tom's finger and let him stroke its neck and exchange friendly chatter. Tom was besotted. So why wouldn't he suspect a parrot for Christmas when he so obviously wanted one?

They're expensive. Their cages are expensive. And, most importantly, parrots have no functional value. Tom can go out and buy himself an eight-cylinder Jeep Grand Cherokee, and he can catalog its many functions: it's a much safer car to commute to Provo in than the Miata; we can haul stuff in it; we can pull a trailer with it; we could get one of those pop-up tents and go camping with it; it can hold our grandkids. He can go on and on this way—although he has more difficulty explaining the leather seats. I know that what he's really saying is, "This is a *man's* car, and a man's gotta have what a man's gotta have. And, hey, it's functional, too."

A parrot, on the other hand, has no useful function. He could not justify to himself spending a heap of money for a parrot that only he really wanted. And he thought I wouldn't buy one either.

Which brings me to the second reason that Tom did not suspect a parrot: I am not a pet person. It's one thing to clean up baby messes; it's quite another thing to clean up after an animal. I made this clear thirty-five years ago when we started our tradition of Sunday afternoon drives in our '61 VW Beetle, and he announced that we would always have dogs.

"I don't want dogs," I said. "We never had a dog or any pet. And I don't want one. I don't know anything about them."

Tom, who had had two setters and a parakeet growing up, said, "Dogs are terrific pets. We have to have dogs."

"I don't want to take care of a dog," I said.

"I'll take care of the dog," he said.

And he did. He has also cared for a monster rabbit, a box turtle, gerbils, and hamsters, once cutting into the drywall to save a hamster from starvation. Our first pet was a singing canary that I wanted to name Elizabeth Ann. We learned at the pet store that only the male birds sing.

"We'll call him Fang," Tom said on the way home.

Poor Fang. He did have a pretty song, but after a while his talons turned black one by one and fell off. He could hardly stand on his perch. Tom soaked his nervous feet in a solution of Epsom salts and made a visit to a veterinarian at a cost more than twice what we paid for the bird and the cage. The vet didn't know any more than we did. Finally, after a courageous battle with rotting feet, Fang died, and Tom buried him outside underneath our living-room window.

Would I do any of these compassionate acts for a hamster or a canary? Would I get out of bed one minute earlier to walk a dog? Not in this life or the life to come. I merely tolerate pets. Tom knew this. He knew I would never voluntarily bring any animal, even a talking bird, into the house, let alone pay a ton of money for one. So there was plenty of opportunity for surprise here.

The third reason he didn't suspect the parrot for Christmas was that we all kept our mouths shut. This was hard for a family of loudmouths. It was especially hard for me not to taunt Tom about the big surprise coming. I'm an enthusiastic taunter. But I didn't do it.

We had some close calls. Once he heard me talking to our son Ed on the phone. "What was that about?" he asked.

"Your Christmas present."

"Something special?"

"No, he just wants to go in on it."

"You're not spending a lot of money, are you?"

"No."

Our friends Ken and Ann knew, because they gave us the name of the parrot breeder. "Ken is a blabbermouth," Ann said. "We have to warn him not to say anything."

I collared Ken at church, and he promised to remain silent.

Then, at the church Christmas party, when Sister K. and I were putting food on the buffet table and Tom was helping, she turned to him and said, "I know what you're getting for Christmas!"

I jumped on her like a rat on a scrap of bacon. "Shhhh!"

"Oh!" She clamped her hand on her mouth.

"What is it?" Tom asked.

Sister K. shook her head.

"Don't even try," I said.

Later, at home, he asked our youngest son, Sam, "What is it?"

"I can't tell you," Sam said.

"You told Sister K.—" Tom prodded.

"Yeah, but I'm not telling you."

On Christmas Eve, the house was filled with the boys and their families. Tom and I fixed and served dinner together. At one point, when we were both in the kitchen, the boys went out and brought in the huge parrot cage and set it in the living room. A note was attached saying that he could choose the parrot himself. When Tom saw it, his jaw dropped. Everyone hooted and whistled. "We got him!" Ed yelled, giving me a high five. Tom was speechless for the first time ever at Christmas. Maybe it was because he'd always wanted a parrot. Maybe it was because we were all so happy to be giving it to him. Maybe it was because he knew the expense. Whatever the case, we did it. We surprised Santa Claus.

Much later that night, when we were lying in bed, I said, "Let's name all the pets we've ever had." And we did:

Fang—canary
Emily—Yorkshire Terrier
Bess—gerbil
You-You I—gerbil (Bess's first husband, maimed)
You-You II—gerbil (Bess's second husband)
Rabbit-Rabbit—rabbit
Katie—hamster

Greg Louganis–goldfish (dove out of fishbowl)

Winnie–Yorkshire Terrier (the second-dumbest dog we ever owned)

T. J.–mongrel (the dumbest dog we ever owned)

Sunshine–parakeet #1

Chickadee–parakeet #2

Greenie–parakeet #3

Maud–Shi Tzu

Spanky–box turtle

Zoe–Bichon Frisé

"What will you name the parrot?" I asked.

He hardly stopped to think about it. "Papagena–from *The Magic Flute*."

I snuggled in. "Were you really surprised? You really didn't know what we were giving you?"

"I didn't know," he said.

"I can hardly believe it. You always figure it out."

"I decided not even to think about it," he said. "I didn't want to figure it out."

So there you have it. Santa Claus is surprised only when he lets you surprise him. Merry Christmas, Santa Claus!

Don't Bite Me, I'm Santa Claus

One winter's night when I was five years old, my mother tucked me in bed and said Santa Claus might come to visit. She'd wake me up if he came, she said. That Santa would actually pay a personal pre-Christmas visit was too much to hope for. Despite the excitement of this wonderful news, I fell asleep. Our old mongrel-Irish-setter, Kelly, lay by my bed that night, both companion and protector.

And a fine protector he was. There was a family story that Kelly had nearly killed the meanest dog on the block when I was sitting on the lawn as an infant. The dog had walked past. Kelly, in his protective mode, had leaped down two terraces of the front lawn, landed squarely on the dog's back, and flattened him on the sidewalk. He ran off yelping and yipping, with Kelly hard on his tail.

I awoke on this night startled by the sound of jingling bells and Kelly's snarling. He dashed out of the bedroom yelping a war cry. I heard him at the front door, his hullabaloo interrupted only by the jingling of bells on the front porch. I ran for the door and arrived just as my mother opened it.

Coming onto the porch was Santa Claus, as real as I could ever hope him to be. Red suit, white fur trim, black boots, rosy cheeks, just like the old Coca Cola ads, and bells jangling. "Ho, ho, ho, merry Christm . . ."

He stopped in mid-consonant and gaped at his nemesis. Kelly charged the screen door. Santa backed up. Kelly charged again, knocking a hole in the screen.

"Kelly," Santa yelled, "don't bite me, I'm . . ." he paused for what seemed a lifetime to a terrified boy, "I'm Santa Claus. I'm Santa Claus!"

Kelly, snarling like a lion, charged again and broke the screen loose. Santa retreated while Kelly, now halfway out the door, tried to push himself through as my mother gripped his midsection to hold him back.

I watched Santa's backside in disbelief as he jostled down the steps, bells jingling, a fat red elf with white curly hair spilling over his collar, a bag filled with presents sailing from my grasp. He would never come back; I was sure of it.

The nausea I felt gave way to rage as I looked at old Kelly, still clawing at the screen door, barking and snarling. I wanted to kill him. My mother was trying to pull him back so she could shut the door, but he would break loose and charge again and again, each time getting a little farther through the screen. He would kill Santa Claus. Santa would die at my house. Santa would be eaten at my house.

At last she won out and shut the door. She scolded the dog. *Bad dog, Kelly, bad dog.* He whimpered and groveled on his belly and rolled on his back, all four legs in the air. Anything she could have said was too mild. No penance could possibly suffice. What do you say to a dog who's destroyed Christmas? He deserved a thrashing. But no one thrashed anyone at my house. So he crept into a corner and lay down, probably confused that anyone would be angry at his defense of the family.

I stood wailing at the disaster that had befallen me. I had enough grief to cry for a thousand years. My mother hugged me and kissed me and wiped away the tears. "Will Santa come back?" I asked through sobs.

"Yes," she said, "but he'll have to sneak in when old Kelly's asleep. He won't come while he's awake. It isn't safe. You'll see. He'll be back."

I was not reassured. How could she know? How could Santa sneak past Kelly? Why would he return to a place where he'd nearly been eaten? Why take a chance like that? I knew what he'd do. He'd go to homes where he'd be safe, and he'd give my presents to other children with nice dogs or no dogs. He was no fool.

My mother took me back to bed. I was still wailing, still disbelieving her promises. She tucked me in and kissed me good night, and Kelly again lay down to protect me. Thanks a whole bunch, Kelly.

When my dad came home from a university party later that evening, I could hear him laughing and sniggering with my mother in the dining room. I drifted off to sleep wondering what could be so funny on a night as terrible as this.

Dear Santa,

Anne and Harrison have requested a new baby for Christmas. This presents a problem, because I don't want a baby for Christmas. They have both been very good this year. I think Harrison only threw one fit per month, down from one fit per day last year. Anne hasn't thrown any fits this year. Her whining has increased, but generally you and I both know they are fabulous children and deserve anything they want for Christmas.

Would a three-year rain check on the baby work? I didn't think so. Okay, then, here's the deal. You finish my university degree and through osmosis give me all the knowledge I would have learned. Then, carry the baby for me. No one would really notice on you anyway. Just make sure you take the prenatal vitamins every day and eat plenty of vegetables and less fat. Also, make sure the baby looks like Charles and me. No offense, but a white beard and a pot belly are not the most becoming features on a baby.

All right, then. We're set. Santa, you're the best! Keep ringing those bells and I'll be waiting for your Christmas package.

> Love,
> Erica, age 22

P.S. Make sure the baby is strapped in a car seat for the sleigh ride.

Dear Santa,

I'll never forget that night so many years ago when I came face-to-face with you. I had been unable to sleep due to the anticipation of your visit and so was not surprised to hear strange sounds coming from the living room.

Fearlessly, I crept out of bed and marched into the room, demanding to know where my pony was. The reply I received was not what an eight-year-old Annie Oakley wanted to hear. I burst into tears.

The next thing I remember is being cradled safely in your ash-stained lap and you attempting to stem my tears. I listened carefully that night, Santa, and have never forgotten what you told me.

With your whiskers tickling my ear, you explained to me the secret of chasing sorrow away by using the magic of laughter. Those ten minutes spent with you while you taught me how to belly laugh were magic for me. I have faithfully practiced your advice all these years.

I have laughed through death, divorce, disease, disappointment, and loneliness. I have thrown my head back as instructed, reached down to my toes, and roared with laughter. MIGHTY LAUGHTER. You were right. An amazing thing does happen when laughter fills your entire being. The sorrows do become bearable, and the joy of life once again fills you.

I have borne the ridicule of people to whom you did not bother to teach this principle, but that was also all right. You guessed it: laughter. Uproarious, out-of-control laughter.

I am getting older and have taught our treasured secret to my son. In turn, I hope he will give Santa's gift to his children. See what you started?

I sleep too heavily now to hear you on your annual visits, but I always leave you my letter reporting the year's activities. As I review the year in writing, I realize that each one is truly more filled with laughter than sorrow. Thank you, Santa.

Now I have just one request. If you are ever ill one year and need a substitute, I would like to apply. I am built just like you, and believe me, I have your belly laugh mastered. Let me know.

Love,
Jeris, age 49

Gravy for Christmas

I have an 8-millimeter home movie of my family on Christmas morning, 1942. Outside the walls of our house, 1942 was a year of turmoil. The country had finally emerged from the Great Depression, but the Japanese had bombed Pearl Harbor scarcely a year before. America had entered the Second World War. By 1942, thousands of American families were mourning the loss of sons and husbands and fathers; others were still stone broke and struggling. Unhappy people were everywhere. There was misery all around our home.

But inside on Christmas morning 1942, there was joy. There was singing. There were gifts galore. My father had managed to work through the entire Depression, at eighty dollars a month, my mother has often reminded me. And from that money they paid a mortgage and fed and clothed themselves, their children, and various of their siblings and parents living in the basement and back rooms. It was enough. My mother's tight-fisted financial management combined with my father's meager salary was enough to see us through and provide gifts for everyone on that Christmas morning.

My parents had asked a friend who owned a movie camera to come and record on film the opening of the gifts. It was a morning when the parents were more excited than the children. Then barely three, still not old enough to awaken early in anticipation of Santa Claus, I was aroused before five in the morning. And the film shows that everyone else in the family was up too: my paternal grandfather and maternal grandmother; my mother and father and sister; my Aunt Beth and Uncle Roscoe.

The now-discolored film shows my ecstatic mother with nimble fingers fitting me into a hand-knit sweater while I rub sleep from my eyes. Then she is setting me on a new rocking horse and rocking me back and forth while I, half-awake, indulge her. What will I call the horse, someone wants to know. "Gravy," I answer without a moment's hesitation. (Now, fifty-three years later, Gravy is an antique rocking horse in my living room.)

After the gifts are opened, the scene changes. My father is standing beside the piano singing while my sister accompanies him. He must be singing "Away in a Manger," because sometimes he looks up and lifts his hand skyward as if singing, "The stars in the heavens"; then he points earthward as if singing, "looked down where he lay." It is better silent; my father sang loudly and off-key. He smiles as he sings, while my sister grins and plays.

The film has become my marker of a life long past and people long gone, a resurrection of memories I lost almost the moment I got them. Without the film I wouldn't remember anything from that day. Of the adults in the film, only Aunt Beth is still alive. My Grandfather Plummer died the next year. My Grandmother Swindle died twenty years later. My father has been dead for thirty-four years. My mother died just a week before Christmas last year, at age ninety-four. My sister is now sixty-six, and I am fifty-eight. Aunt Beth is well into her eighties. And the house, where the family lived for more than sixty years, was sold two months ago.

On Christmas, three days after Mother's funeral, the family wanted to see pictures. I watched the film again with my wife, my sons, and their wives. Grandchildren looked on with curious faces as their parents would say, "Look, there's Grandpa when he was a little boy. That's his mom rocking him on Gravy. And there's Great-grandpa Plummer." My sons never knew him. Of all the images, only Gravy is recognizable, although his mane is gone, cut off by our youngest son, Sam, when he was three. It was the only time in his life that I spanked him.

Only Gravy remains to remind me, as I walk into my living room, of a magical time that somehow, ever so imperceptibly, slipped from grasp. And Santa has become a measure of the ceaseless spinning and unraveling of my life into old age. Doctors talk of getting a baseline on blood pressure, cholesterol, and heart function. Santa Claus is my emotional baseline. And, sadly, he reminds me that if I want magic, I must create it myself. I must stand behind the set like the Wizard of Oz and operate the buttons and levers without any help from those before me.

Dear Santa,

I would like it a lot if I could have all my horses and cats and a few of my favorite cows come back to life. I loved them and I miss them and I would like to feed them and pet them and call them by their names and have them come to me to get rubbed in their favorite rubbing places. I think what I really would like is to see my parents and brother who have gone away. And some aunts and uncles and grandparents.

Next, I would like to have a big cattle ranch in the Wind Rivers in Wyoming, and I would like it to be right by the House Rock Valley in northern Arizona, so all I would have to do is to move the cattle up into the mountains in Wyoming every spring and let them drift back to the desert in the fall. I would need a few bales of hay for my horses, but none for the cows. I could buy the hay for the horses, so there would be no irrigating and no hay to put up. Just riding and watching the new calves and moving the cattle onto fresh feed and packing salt up onto the ridges to keep the cattle from hanging down on the bottoms and chewing out all the grass there. The bad thing about that is that I would never want to sell any of the calves, because someone would want to kill them to eat. So, Santa, just forget the whole ranch idea, and I will try to forget it too, knowing all the while that I never will forget. Like the horses and cows and cats, ranches will forever tug at my soul.

Oh, and please don't be offended that I told my grandson Adam that you were only a story people tell children. And don't worry about him. Two weeks after I told him there was no Santa Claus, he told his mother that every year Abraham Lincoln rises up to bring toys to all the children for Christmas. Turns out it's all in the beard.

Bob, age 71

Dear Santa,

This year I don't want a horse, but please send me a grandchild. Send it through my daughter and her husband. They have been trying to have a baby for many years. Then on Christmas mornings they can have a child who can open your presents. This seems more reasonable than my horse did, right?

Santa, I also need a doll, a doll for my younger daughter. She needs to be adored. And frankly, that's all I want the doll to do—adore her. I know you make a popular Ken doll. He's the one that is tall and handsome, but I suspect that's all he is. So make one with great looks and a great body if you'd like, but make certain this doll has a huge heart.

I also have two sons, one twenty-two and one sixteen. The older one needs a stocking full of confidence, not candy and nuts. He thinks he needs a girl, but we both know she wouldn't fit in his stocking. I think confidence that he is capable and bright is what he needs this year. Give it to me, and I will make sure it finds its way into his stocking.

The younger one, well, the younger one is sixteen, and you know that at that age they need just about everything. I know "everything" is difficult to do, even for you, but let's just try this: send him the gift of happiness. He is a happy boy, always has been. But make it a perpetual gift. It doesn't need fancy wrapping and bows. The gift itself is exquisite.

Now, Santa, I always wanted to have a horse. You never gave me one, and I must admit that I was disappointed. But then you really outdid yourself and gave me a great gift when I was twenty-two. You gave me light. The light has burned brightly since then, in me and in my daughters and sons. It is bright all the time, even when I'm dark. The light is also warm. I feel it every day and night. So do others.

The light has been dimmed lately. It has been beaten up by cancer and then by chronic fatigue syndrome. I don't think I ever would want to be without this warmth and light. Send my wife the light, C.G.H. This is not as well known as many of your other gifts, but it is what she needs. It's Chronic Good Health.

Well, Santa, that's it. No horses this year, but it's okay. It's what I would like.

Rick, age 50

Who Was That Bearded Man?

Several years ago in Minnesota on Christmas Eve, on my first foray as Santa Claus, I tied several pillows around my chest and derriere, put on the requisite red suit, black boots, beard, wig, and red hat, and waddled down the street to the home of our neighbors Gordon and Lanay Davis. They were having a formal Christmas dinner party with twelve people.

Gordon, not knowing who I was, admitted me nonetheless because I was Santa Claus. He introduced me into the dining room, where guests, in the middle of the second course, greeted me with cheers.

I had a bag full of candy kisses, which I distributed to the party guests amidst gaiety and smarty remarks. I kissed all the women, who puckered right up without so much as a question mark, and hugged a couple of guys, who laughed tensely. After a few jokes, I jostled on out the door. Gordon, in the meantime, had seen through the layers of costume to identify me, but Lanay had not. When I was gone, she said, "Who was that guy, anyway?"

Now, there's tremendous power in this anonymity. First, people are confused when Santa Claus appears unexpectedly at their house. They know there's probably someone inside the outfit whom they know. *Probably*—but not for sure. And if the costume is good, they don't know who it is, anyway. And since they don't know who it is, they don't know what this particular Santa knows about their life—and foibles. This makes Santa a loose cannon. What will he say? Will he disclose their skeletons hidden away in some forgotten or suppressed closet? Will he embarrass them? Of course, a good Santa doesn't do any of that. That's a violation of the Christmas spirit. But he can have some fun with them.

Such an occasion occurred during the Christmas season last year. My sister- and brother-in-law, Marilyn and Neil van Keizerswaard, were having a little dinner party with a neighbor couple. Neil had access to Dutch Sinter Klaas and Swarte Piet outfits that his parents had bought during a visit to Holland. Would I, they asked, play Sinter Klaas, and they'd have their young son, Michael, dressed up as Swarte Piet, a little minstrel-looking sidekick to Sinter Klaas who punishes bad kids by stuffing them in his bag and spinning them around.

"I don't know anything about being Sinter Klaas," I said. "And I can't speak Dutch or even fake a Dutch accent."

"That doesn't matter," Marilyn said. "Just be funny."

On the appointed date, I entered their house through the garage door, carrying my costume in a big bag. As I passed through a back room I found myself looking straight into the eyes of one of the guests, whose face I recognized from someplace or other. He didn't even seem to notice me. I couldn't remember where I had met him. It was like being at a community picnic and seeing someone who cashiers at the grocery store. You can't quite figure out in the new context who the person is.

I went downstairs, where Michael was being dressed by his sister, and began putting on the Sinter Klaas outfit. It's pretty much like a Santa Claus getup, except that you wear a robe on top of the red suit and a hat that makes you look like the Archbishop of Canterbury.

As I was dressing, I finally remembered who the man was. I had met him at a BYU football game about two weeks before. BYU was playing its archrival, the University of Utah, and he had come to the game with my cousin Art Swindle and had sat next to us. Art, an employee and staunch supporter of the University of Utah, had never sat in the BYU stadium before, and neither had his friend, who was also from rival-land. Now I remembered that his name was Bill Hansen. In the course of the game, through small talk, I had learned that Bill was an attorney in Salt Lake, that he occasionally taught a law course at BYU, that he had certain interests in law that I remembered before Christmas but don't remember now.

Thus armed with the advantage of my disguise and some facts about Bill, I went upstairs with Swarte Piet. Marilyn whispered the name of Lori, Bill's wife, to me on the way up. We got the usual response. Even when you have only four people present and two know what's going on, everyone whoops. Marilyn introduced me to the guests. I kissed her and Lori, gave the guys a hug, used a German accent (which I *can* imitate) to fake a Dutch one, and we were all jovial. Then, bit by bit, as I spoke, I let out information that I could recall about Bill from the football game.

Now everyone but me was on slippery ground. Neil and Marilyn didn't know that I had sat next to him; he had no idea who I was or how I might have come up with facts about him; and, being a lawyer, he had naturally become a little suspicious. I asked him a couple of things about his law practice, and asked his wife a thing or two about his ethics. Neil and Marilyn were wondering how on earth I knew so much, and the Hansens were noticeably impressed. After a few photos I returned to the basement, changed clothes, and slipped out the back door. I laughed to myself all the way home, where I told Louise what I'd done, and we laughed a whole lot more.

I learned later from Neil and Marilyn that Bill immediately began asking who I was. After some prodding, Marilyn confessed that I was her brother-in-law.

"What's his name?"

"Tom Plummer."

"Plummer. Plummer. That's Art Swindle's cousin. I sat next to him at the football game last month," he said. "That's how he knew so much."

Pity. He might have become a believer.

Dear Santa,

You've been great to me for many years. You've given me lots of stuff. Thank you.

But this year I'm asking that you don't give me any more stuff. I have plenty. Probably too much. This year I'm asking that instead of giving me stuff, you give me the answer to one question: How do you get so much done in one night?

I have to know. I used to think you were just fast. But then I figured that speed couldn't be the answer, because if you went as fast as I calculate you'd have to go, carrying the weight you'd have to carry, the friction would disintegrate you and your reindeer on takeoff.

So it has to be something else. I'm guessing you've figured out how to slow down or stop time. *I need to know how to do that!*

I need to stop time just long enough to get caught up, to take care of the piles of papers stacked on my desk and on the floor, to read what I must read, to write what I must write, to get my house and yard in shape, to check everything off my "To Do" list. To take an uninterrupted nap.

And then when I'm caught up I'll start time again and I'll spend it doing the things I've always wanted to do: playing with my kids, talking with my friends, taking long, unhurried walks to nowhere. These are things I never seem to have time for now. Help me.

Desperately seeking time,
Rick, age 41

P.S. You know my address
Home Phone: 801—555—2524
Office Phone: 801—555—2222
Toll Free: 1—800—866—6824
Cell phone: 801—555—7425
Pager: 801—555—9999
Fax: 801—555—4357
Web site: www.2much2do.com
E-mail: rick@2much2do.com

P.P.S. If you can't tell me your secret, could you at least bring me a couple dozen clones?

Dear Santa,

I haven't checked in with you in forty years or so, because I have learned that by talking incessantly for months, I can usually get what I want for Christmas from other sources. So I've tried to make your load a bit lighter. Nevertheless, I have always remembered you and often left milk and cookies.

But this year, dear Santa, my husband and I are in need.

For your adult petitioners, do you have a home repairs division? Elves skilled in the building trades? In July we married and bought what we thought was a beautiful home, built by a contractor who had lived in it himself for nine years. Although he may have built fine houses for others, his standard for his own seems to have been, "That'll do." Basically, we find ourselves in danger of flood.

We need:

Foundation experts—water seeps into the basement rooms along the east side of the house. What are we supposed to do to stop that?

Plumbers and carpet layers—the water heater rusted through in the night and leaked its entire hundred gallons onto the new carpet in the downstairs bedroom.

More plumbers and plasterers—the cooler in the roof was apparently installed incorrectly, because after we had used it for a couple of weeks, water began leaking through the ceiling, softening the plaster and dripping from the beams into our lovely living room.

Roofers—the former owner says that the boards on the roof change the direction of the wind just enough to keep it from blowing off shingles. But should we have to have large boards on our roof? And how many shingles have we already lost? Will the roof leak when the snows start?

Sprinkling system experts—the pipes and valves and tiny knobs of each watering point look like they were designed by a distracted scientist. They break if you touch them with a tiny bit too much force. At this moment we have a four-foot fountain of bubbling water flooding the lawn and the fields because someone threw a hose instead of moving it gently, and it snapped in half the flimsy, child's-toy-plastic pipe where it connected. We've had a four-foot fountain for five days. We don't know how to turn the water off.

Santa, if you could get those elves here now, you might save us from floating away.

As for whether we deserve the assistance, don't you think it shows our courage and belief in life that we've married at forty-eight? And even if you can't help us and we break away in the flood and float off our foundation in our own personal ark, we will still love each other deeply, gather the dogs and kids around us, and hold on.

                    With a lot of hope,
                    Susan, age 48

P.S. If you don't have a home repairs division, would you consider starting one? Immediately?

Santa Has Truth Serum

Santa gets the truth out of people like no one else can. No parent, no teacher, not even a cop can do it as well. People lie to authorities, but they don't lie to Santa.

I realized this one Christmas Eve when I was shoveling snow at our house in St. Paul, Minnesota, and asked my son Jonathan to bring me an ice scraper. An early-morning storm had dumped several inches, and I was working quickly to clear the walks and driveway before they turned into a holiday hazard. Procrastinators in Minnesota find themselves walled off from the rest of the world and must wait until spring to come outside again.

Jonathan was on the roof of the house. Maybe he was shoveling off snow; maybe he was fooling around. I didn't want him up there because asphalt shingles become brittle in cold weather, and tromping around on the roof damages them. Having him fetch an ice scraper was a good way to get him off.

"Get it yourself," he said. "I'm on the roof."

"Yes, I can see that, but I don't want you on the roof. I want you to get off and get the ice scraper."

Jonathan could be belligerent in the face of authority. "No," he said. "I'm not getting your stupid ice scraper."

"Get off the roof and get the ice scraper, or there's going to be trouble," I yelled.

He was fully up to the challenge. "Drop dead, you %#$@*#+@," he replied. In his adolescent years, Jonathan had acquired an astonishing vocabulary.

Considering the time of year and the damage I could do to the family's celebration of Christmas, I backed off. Reluctantly. Besides, getting even appealed even more. Jonathan had just joined Santa's "naughty" list. If I didn't have power with Jonathan, Santa did. "You'd better not pout, you'd better not cry, you'd better not shout, I'm telling you why . . ." La de de da da de da.

Jonathan and I kept clear of each other for the rest of the day. Distance was the only safe thing. Restraint. For just a few more hours.

Evening came. I slipped off to don my suit. Louise piled up gifts outside the front door, hoping no one would run out and find them before I was ready. Grandma Plummer, who was visiting from Salt Lake City, sat warming herself by the fire. I sneaked out the back door, through several feet of Minnesota snow, and onto the porch. I rang the bell.

"Go see who's there, Jonathan," I heard Louise say. Jonathan answered the door and looked at me with doubting eyes.

"Hello there, young fella," I said. "Are you by any chance Jonathan Plummer?"

"Yes," he said. His tone was cold.

"Well, I'm Santa Claus," I said. "How about a big hug?"

He hesitated, and then reached out and hugged me with limp arms.

"Now, that's not a hug," I said. "Let's have a real hug for old Santa, or I might have to give your presents to someone else."

He hugged hard. I hugged hard. I looked beyond Jonathan to see his little brothers dancing around yelling, "It's Santa

Claus, it's Santa Claus!" Behind them I could see the vague forms of Louise and my mother, laughing and becoming children. They were vague forms because I had taken off my glasses to camouflage my identity, and that meant I could see next to nothing.

"Ho, ho, ho," I said, dragging the big bag of presents and Gravy, the rocking horse, into the house. "If this is the Plummer family, I have a whole pile of stuff for you."

"This is the place," Louise said.

"Well, where do you want me to sit?" I asked.

"How about over here on the hearth?" Louise said. A blazing fire, a big tree, and a couple of hundred pounds of presents ensured that this was going to be a good Christmas.

"First," I said, "let's have the old people. Where's your dad?" The kids looked around and shrugged their shoulders.

"He went out for a few minutes," Louise said.

"Well, let's have this little lady here," I said, pointing to my mother. Her four-foot-eight, eighty-five-pound frame was shaking like a Model T Ford. "Come up here and sit on Santa's lap."

A photo from that night shows her sitting on Santa's lap, mouth wide open, one hand trying to hold in her false teeth, which tended to slip out when she laughed too hard.

"Elva, have you been a good girl?" I asked, putting as much sternness into my tone as I could muster.

"Yes, Santa," she said. "I'm always a good girl. I don't do bad things."

"You don't look like a troublemaker," I said. "Are you sure you're telling me the truth? You haven't been even a little bit naughty all year?"

"No, Santa," she replied. "I've been just as nice as can be all year."

I picked up her present and tried to read the label. Without glasses, I could barely see it. I held the package up to my face, squinting, struggling to read the note. This brought even more laughing. Finally I could make out the words *Grandma Plummer*. "Yup, this is for you," I said and turned her loose.

Louise got the same treatment and assured me she too had been a good girl.

And now it was Jonathan's turn. He came reluctantly, as teenagers do when they are trying to act cool, but he sat on my lap.

"Now, Jonathan," I said. "Have you been a good boy?"

"Yup," he said.

"Well, let's see," I said. "How are you doing in school?"

"A's and B's," he said.

"Hmmm. That's mighty fine," I said. "Do you read your scriptures and say your prayers?"

"Mostly," he said.

"Mostly." I stroked my beard. "How often is mostly? Once a day? Once a week? Once a month? Help me out here, son."

I could feel him twitch.

"More than once a week," he said.

"Hmmm," I said. "Are you good to your dear mother and handsome father?"

He hesitated. "Mostly," he said.

"Do you always do what you're asked to do?"

"Mostly."

"When your dad asks you to get an ice scraper for him, do you get it? Be careful now, son. It's important you tell the truth. Santa can see the truth in your eyes."

He paused and looked at me with a funny grin. "I didn't today," he said.

"Why not?"

"I didn't want to."

"Well, son," I continued, "did you say that in a kind way to your father, your hard-working father who loves you so much?"

"Kinda," he said.

"Now, Jonathan," I said very slowly. "I don't think you saw me, but I was sitting in the tree behind you when you said something naughty to your dear father. Do you remember what it was?"

"Yes," he said. He was squirming.

"Can you tell me what you said?"

"No."

"Why not?"

"'Cause it's a naughty word."

"You can whisper it in my ear."

"No, I don't want to say it," he said.

"Well, if I said it, would you recognize it?"

"Yes."

"Should I say it?"

"No."

"But you won't say it either?"

"No."

"Are you ever going to say it again?"

"I don't know."

"Let's try that once more. Are you ever going to say it again?"

"I guess not," he said.

"Well, I hope not. That was not a nice thing to say to your father, was it?"

"Nope."

"Well, I think I can give you your present now," I said. I handed him a big box. "Can you say, 'Thank you, Santa Claus'?"

"Thanks, Santa."

"Would you give Santa a big kiss on the cheek?"

He groaned. I leaned forward toward him. He kissed my cheek.

When I am Santa, I am powerful. More powerful than a father. More powerful than police. I wonder if police wouldn't have better luck interrogating people if they wore Santa suits and gave a little present to everyone who tells the truth.

Dear Santa,

Every Christmas for some twenty years, I asked that you pull some strings and fulfill one of my fantasies by getting me the role of Clara in the *Nutcracker*. A couple of decades ago, after years of disappointment, I gracefully gave up on the notion with the theory that perhaps I didn't look eleven years old any more. I moved on to the monumental dream that I could star as the Sugarplum Fairy. I asked that in addition to swinging the deal, you would bring me the necessary equipment, which included a pink tutu, a pair or two of size 7 toe shoes, some serious support hose, and a couple of knee replacements to increase my chances of managing the famous Sugarplum Fairy solo, as well as some silicone implants to round things out.

What happened? Absolutely nothing. I'm afraid you stonewalled me, Santa. This year I'm going to give you one more chance to prove you are not a total deadbeat. Lest you think me too much of a Walter Mitty, I am offering a reasonable and realistic alternative to Clara or Sugarplum Fairy. This year I would like you to bring me a contract for the role of Mother Buffoon. This will cover a number of worrisome problems. The pantaloons (which you will need to bring me) will be great for covering a terminal case of varicose veins, and the billowing skirts I am asking for will camouflage a billowing belly. Also, the mask, or, actually, headgear she always wears will negate the need for a facelift, which was part of my hidden agenda.

All in all, it looks like the perfect compromise to my long-held visions of grandeur. Santa, while I appreciate any possible efforts you may have expended in past years on my behalf, I do hope this will be the year that you prove you are worth your salt.

Best regards,
Connie, age 53

P.S. If all else fails, I need a new vacuum. One of my favorite sounds is the whirring of the vacuum off in the distance, heralding the fact that for once, someone else is doing the work. Maybe you could even con one of my teenage sons into running it for me occasionally.

Dear Santa:

I would like a hearing Christmas. Last Christmas I could hear. Now I can't. Fifty years ago I lost the hearing in my left ear because of infections. This was not a big deal, since I had a good ear with normal hearing. Five months ago, my good ear became not very good at all.

I have a hearing aid in that ear which doesn't work very well. The audiologist tries and tries, but it seems I am the problem rather than the hearing aid. I had surgery to improve the hearing in my left ear last month. It didn't work. Just after getting the hearing aid, I was outside with Virginia (my wife, you'll remember). I heard an unpleasant, indefinable screeching noise. Ginny said it was just a bird chirping. When we go for walks, the wind in the trees sounds like a strange motor, and the sound of water flowing in the stream is a grating noise.

A world in which the sounds of birds chirping, streams flowing, and wind blowing in the aspens are unpleasant is a forbidding, alien place. I would like my old world back.

I can't hear people very well, either. In fact, my own voice is unfamiliar to me. The sound of me has been altered so that I am not sure who is forming words, or how loudly. Am I shouting? Or speaking too softly? I can't tell. I can probably eventually adjust to this new world of silence and noise, but I would still like my old world back.

I have to admit that in years past, I didn't much care for Christmas carols, at least for what we do with them. Beginning in November, and continuing until the moment of Christmas, carols in elevators, grocery stores, department malls, and telephone waiting would grate on me until I vowed I would become the Christmas Carol Midnight Skulker. I fantasized about sneaking into public places and disconnecting speaker wires, disabling tape and CD players to quell the endless aural assault. This Christmas I won't do that.

In fact, if I could have a hearing Christmas, I would never again grumble about nonstop carols. I used to have a good ear for music. Now music is as unpleasant as the burbling brook. I would like to enjoy music again. I will shortly have surgery to try to improve the hearing in my right ear. The adult in me tells me that you can't help, and this letter is foolish. There is enough child left in me to ask anyway.

> Sincerely,
> Al, age 59

P.S. Don't worry about the reindeer making too much noise on the roof. For me, at least, it won't matter. I wouldn't hear them if they came *through* the roof.

Timbales for Santa

When I was a child, my family set out treats for Santa Claus every Christmas Eve. Watching my mother and grandmother doing the Christmas baking, keeping recipes incredibly in their heads, using their hands and fingers as measuring cups and spoons, moving their fingers nimbly to mix and knead dough, was like watching magicians.

My mother allowed me to choose some of their finest goods for Santa Claus—chocolate chip or carrot cookies, thickly frosted brownies full of walnuts, and always a little fruitcake. I would set the plate ceremoniously on the dining-room table along with a note to Santa Claus, a last-minute reminder of what I had asked him to bring.

During my adolescent years, my mother learned how to make Swedish timbales by dipping a hot iron shaped like a butterfly or snowflake into a thin batter and deep-frying it. The batter turns light brown, and the grooves in the cooled butter-fly or snowflake can be laced with frosting—my mother used red and green for Christmas—or sprinkled with powdered sugar.

Timbales are a labor-intensive treat. You can make only one or two at a time. Without enough batter on the iron, the tim-bale comes out too thin and breaks apart. Too much batter, and it molds to the form and comes off only when broken. If you leave it in the hot oil just a moment too long, it turns a dark, inedible brown. If you apply frosting, you must neatly line it onto the timbale with a hand-held applicator, squeezing out frosting with one hand while guiding the nozzle with the other. My timbales looked like freeway accidents, while Mother's were neatly finished.

Sometimes, after a day's work, she'd have a whole stack of timbales, and a visitor would come into the kitchen, usually a big guy who had no idea of what sacrifice had gone into the making, grab a couple of fists full, and wolf them down. "Mmmmm, these are great," he'd say, grabbing one handful after another. One man ate the entire day's work, blabbering on about nothing while he stuffed it all away.

Although this drove Mother crazy, she would say not a word to him about his piggishness. "I'm glad you like them," she'd say. Later, after he'd left, brushing timbale crumbs onto the floor from his shirt and pants, she'd say, "Laws, did you see that? He ate my whole platter of timbales. Now I'll have to start all over."

For me, the joy of leaving treats for Santa was the anticipation of his personal reply, which I would find under the empty plate on the table on Christmas morning. I still have a note from Christmas 1946:

My dear little Tommy,

I was glad to learn that you were asleep when I came along. Some kids were awake and that did not go over well with me. I gave one kid a few spanks and left no toys at all because he acted so smart. Smarty kids give me a pain in the neck.

Well, Tom, I got the things you needed and wanted but I must ask you for a little cooperation, how about it? I know you will do what I ask so I am going to leave all you asked for and more too. But, note this. I want you to share the tools with your dad and Uncle Roscoe. Let them use them when they want to. If your little sister wants to borrow your radio at times, let her take it. I don't think she has one, or at least if she has it is not a very good one. Don't let her trade hers for yours or you will be a sucker.

I left two vises, one for your dad and one for you. You can take the one you want and give him the other or if you and your dad can work it out and use them both on the same bench o.k. By the way, I could not find a decent bench, so get your Uncle Roscoe to help you make one. If you can get your dad to help you boys, o.k., but if he is too tired, don't bother him. He is a rather tired man. Your mother is sure a cute little trick. I gave her a big kiss for you. She made me some coffee and toast. I am very tired. I had to come in this big truck.

Well, Tom, be a nice boy and have a good time. I hope you will enjoy shoveling some snow this winter with that fine shovel.

Santa Claus

Now I recognize my father's ironic tone. He liked words like *sucker* and *smarty*. Still, the notes did not arouse my suspicion so much as assure me that Santa Claus was just as kind, just as enamored with my mother, and just as twisted as my father was. How could I be so fortunate that Santa Claus was a lot like him?

Dear Santa,

You have brought the magic of Christmas ever since I was a little girl.

You have brought other things, too. I loved the blue-eyed doll with the nightgown that matched mine. I wondered about those scraps in the wastebasket. The flowered flannel seemed like a strange choice for Dad's new pajamas, which is where Mom told me it came from. And you gave me a great bike one year. We were locked out of the basement for days while paint smells wafted through the door. Do you help all dads paint bikes, or just mine? I think my favorite present was the stack of new library books. The best one was *Seventeenth Summer.* I was thirteen when you brought that book, but I pretended to be seventeen all the while I read it.

Your attention didn't stop with childhood. Thanks for tracking us down the year we tried to surprise Grandma and Grandpa by flying across the country on Christmas Eve with our four little children. All of our luggage was lost, but there were still stockings with oranges in the toes on Christmas morning. By evening, you had dropped a generous round of gifts. I'm sorry we confused you at the last minute.

There was the year we were without a job and thought you might skip our house. But you arrived on schedule with a few very carefully chosen presents, thanks to some of your kind helpers. We busied ourselves that year doing the Twelve Days of Christmas for an immigrant family who *really* had nothing. Each evening we would put together a little package of trinkets or a plate of cookies and drop it at their door. Through the window we could see their excitement. We felt the spirit of Christmas in a new way that year and learned that what we *got* didn't have much to do with happiness. Thank you for that great gift.

How you managed last year is still a mystery. With all of our family home (8), plus Grandpa (1), plus our son-in-law's family (7), plus their Russian "son" (1), plus our Brazilian friends (5), we had a real house full. How did you shop for 22 pairs of pajamas? By the way, they all fit. I thought you might like this picture of all the kids (15) on the stairs on Christmas morning. Thanks for making it such a party.

Through the years we have moved, grown, changed. Thanks for staying the same. No matter what happens during the year, your visit on Christmas Eve brings back the childlike trust that tells us someone knows where we are, knows what we need, and wants to make us happy. Now that the children are grown up, I wonder each year if it will be your last visit. Or will you still come when I am ninety-five like the Grandpa who lives with us? He always says he doesn't want anything, and if he needs something he'll get it himself. But I think he secretly likes it that you still come. I think I will too.

Belated thanks and love,
Betsy, age 55

Dear Santa,

There was a time when I believed in magic. I was younger then. At Christmas I always got what I wanted. My mother said it was because I knew what to ask for, and I didn't ask for impossible things. This year I want to ask for impossible things, things of childhood, things that require magic.

Help my children and the children of the world to feel safe, as safe as I felt when my father would let me climb into his lap, and he would wrap his strong arms around me and make everything all right again. I knew without a doubt that there would be no pain or sorrow too big to hold within the circle of that love. But he died too young.

Give my children and the children of the world the wonder and excitement of discovery I felt as I sat beside my mother as she read stories to me. I learned of other places and other times, and my world grew with the magic of words through my mother's deep alto voice. She is now old, and her deep alto voice is shaky. I try to care for her the same way she cared for me, because I remember the magic she shared with me.

Give children laughter, the pure innocent uncontrolled laughter of youth. Let them be able to share that laughter and the healing it brings.

Let children know the magic of love. When they look in the mirror, let that reflection be from the eyes of all who love them. Help them to give freely of their love so that they learn that love multiplies as it is given away.

> Love,
> Ginny, age 57

Value Past,
Value Present

Every Christmas of my boyhood, my Grandmother Swindle gave me a year's subscription to Walt Disney's *Comics and Stories* and a gift box with twelve rolls of Life Savers. The total cost to her, if memory serves me correctly, was $1.60: one dollar for the subscription and sixty cents for the Life Savers. She would hand her gift to me with trembling hands and say, "It isn't much, but it's all I can give."

I knew that. My grandmother lived with our family because she had had a heart attack at age sixty and had little money to care for herself. She moved in when I was three years old. For as long as I could remember, she had moved slowly and somewhat unsteadily. Her hands shook with age, and her head bobbed. She raised money for gifts to the family on birthdays and Christmas by crocheting handkerchiefs, which she sold for $1.60 each to Mormon Handicraft, a store in downtown Salt Lake City. She'd start with a small square of linen that had perforations around the edges, and, using a fine white thread and a tiny crochet hook, create an intricate border about an inch wide around the linen. Because the thread was so fine and the weave so delicate, each handkerchief took her several days to complete.

This was all the more daunting because of her fading eyesight from macular degeneration and her palsied hands, but she persisted. "I have to do my part," she would say. She'd sit in an overstuffed rocker brought to her room from the old homestead in Monroe, Utah. She rocked ever so gently as her hands articulated the thread slowly into a pattern as delicate as snowflakes.

Her poverty was a lifelong blight. My mother's autobiography recounts how people in Monroe "made do" in the early part of the twentieth century:

> Father always went to the mountains and got our Christmas tree. We spent hours stringing cranberries,

popcorn, and making red and green chains to cover the fresh pine boughs. Our whole house smelled of its fragrance. We didn't have much money, but I never can forget how grateful we were for the presents we received. Our stockings always had an orange in the toe. It was only once a year our store carried oranges. It was a celebration in itself. I always kept mine so long I either had to eat it or lose it. We counted our candy and nuts to see that Santa treated us all equally.

So when I received this small gift from my grandmother, I knew what lay behind it. It didn't occur to me to complain that she had not spent much money; her gift, in terms of hours spent, was probably the most expensive of any I ever received.

For all its emotional value, I realize now, ironically, that her gift also would have had the greatest monetary value if I'd had the foresight of hindsight. Sitting on my bed, I read and reread the comic books, the stories of Donald and Daisy Duck and nephews Huey, Dewey, and Louie, of Uncle Scrooge, of Mickey and Minnie Mouse, of Pluto and Goofy—both dogs, but only one could speak. And I waited each month for the next issue to see how the serial mystery at the end of each comic would continue or end.

Now I wish I'd taken one of the dollars I'd received from someone else and gotten a second subscription of Walt Disney's *Comics and Stories* to keep in an airtight, acid-free box for collectors at a later time. Out of curiosity, I called a comic book store in Salt Lake City to ask what such comics would be worth today if they were in mint condition.

"Depending on condition and issue," the man on the phone said, "ten cents to who knows how much."

He was anticipating, I'm sure, that these would not be in mint condition, since no one—at least not anyone like me—keeps them unopened in an airtight, acid-free storage box. But I persisted. "Well, let's say they really are in perfect condition. How much is 'who knows how much'?"

"Who knows?" he said.

"C'mon, you must be able to put some value on it. Give me a figure off the top of your head."

"Twenty dollars," he said.

So, $20 x 12 issues x 10 years = $24,000. That, invested for ten years at 10 percent, would come to $62,250. Invested for ten years at 15 percent, it could come to $97,093. I sit here amazed at lost opportunities that my grandmother had, quite unconsciously, pointed me toward. Had I put away a duplicate of her one-dollar present and sold the duplicate now, my retirement would look quite a bit rosier. No other present that I ever received in my childhood, except for my rocking horse, Gravy, and my dangerous-to-your-health lead soldiers, has accumulated value over the years, and nothing has become so valuable by far as those comic books.

But that's all fantasy stuff. I didn't buy an extra subscription and save the issues in an airtight, acid-free box. In fact, acid-free boxes are a recent invention.

In the end, what remains important is the memory of my grandmother's persistent sacrifice to make one crocheted handkerchief each year to buy me a Christmas present. Thank you, Grandma-Santa.

Dear Santa,

You made the world a better place
For us when we were small.
Longed-for treasures came into view
With no foul-up at all.
How did you do it? By magic?
We need to learn your art—
Getting each load in place, on time,
Without falling apart.
You've been our shining example.
You get things done on time.
You sack-up, drop-off and move on.
You can stop on a dime.
We need some of your expertise.
We cannot work alone.
Let's look to modern science—the
Miracle of the clone.
Santa, if you would clone yourself,
You'd see yourself around.
One Santa for each family—
Mirth and joy would be found
To lift and brighten our spirits
And fill each heart with cheer.
Santa, could we possibly start
At Christmastime—this year?

Florence, age 88

Dear Santa,

You of all people know how often I move, so I think you'll understand why I don't want anything too big or permanent this year. At this point I'm still using crates as furniture, and besides my bed nothing I own has cost me over $40. I'm trying to simplify my life a bit, so I'm only asking for what I really need. Like chocolate (dark, please).

Also, you may have heard that I've taken up rock climbing, and just like camping, hiking, running, and the other things I do to enjoy the great outdoors, it's really all about the gear. So for Christmas this year I'd love any useful equipment with lots of compartments, zippers, straps, etc.—preferably made from metallic or brightly colored synthetic materials originally designed for space travel.

If there's anything left in the budget, I'd love the balance in diesel gas stations (it's the fuel of the future—why am I the only driver in the greater Los Angeles basin with a '98 diesel automobile?!).

Finally, if it's not too much trouble, could you drop off a grandkid at my parents' house? My brothers and sister and I would really appreciate it.

> Thanks, Santa!
> Becca, age 26

Attention, Catalog Shoppers

At some point after our older kids lost faith in Santa Claus (that dark period of doubt and cynicism between childhood and adulthood), we became weary of shopping for their every Christmas desire. They'd tell us the longings of their hearts, and we, like golden retrievers, would search the malls to find just the right thing. But we just couldn't get it right. We'd buy cheap imitations of the requested toys, clothes that weren't cool, electronic games off the mark. "I said Donkey Kong, not Bongo Long."

We'd watch their faces for some sign of joy as they opened our Christmas gifts, for indications of gratitude that would validate us as parents. But they, like other kids, had their own codes to live by, one of them being never to let their parents think that the desires of their palpitating little hearts had been satisfied. They had solemn obligations to this code of ethics, maybe sworn around dripping candles in dark caves, never to show their parents that they were truly happy about any gift.

Finally, after a particularly disappointing Christmas of race cars that wouldn't run; jeans with a little teeny stamp on the label that said *IRREGULAR*—"They're gonna tease me and say I'm IRREGULAR, wah wah wah wah wah"; white ice skates from Marnie's Used Skate and Sled Shop—"I can't show up at the hockey rink with white skates, I'll be killed"; sometime in the early 1980s, Louise and I had a little time alone. "Next year," she said, "let's give them a LaBelle's catalog and let them pick out their own presents. That way they can't complain about their gifts, and we'll just call in their order."

At that gloomy moment it seemed like a pretty good idea. We would thrust the responsibility for Christmas onto their shoulders, make them accountable for their own Christmas joy. They couldn't complain then. They could only feel some pleasure that Santa Claus—repellent as the myth now was to them—at least had tastes like their own. This had the feeling of

a correct principle of child rearing. It rang of real consequences, that foundation of child psychology that assumes that
children can be raised properly if parents just understand how
to apply natural and logical consequences to misbehavior. We
were to learn that these psychologists had not spent Christmas
at our house. Our plan, we were to learn, step by painful step,
had disaster written all over it.

"How do we control costs?" I asked.

"We'll set a price limit and let them choose what they want
in that range," she said. "Then we just pick up the phone. No
Christmas shopping. No crowd busting."

"Okay," I said, "anything's worth a try."

So when the LaBelle's Christmas catalog arrived in early
October, we announced the plan. We gathered them into a
solemn little circle, looked them in the eye, and told them they
could browse through the catalog for anything up to a speci-
fied price (a figure that Louise and I reached with considerable
tension and argument). They would decide their Christmas
presents and therefore live and be happy with them.

"Can we get more than one thing if they all add up to that
price?" someone wanted to know.

"Yes."

"Does the price have to include sales tax?"

"Yes," I said.

"No," Louise said. "They can't figure out sales tax. Just let them ask for what they want before tax. We can pay the tax."

My stomach clenched, even as the words of my friend Gordon Davis rang in my ears: "You have to choose your fights. Pick the big fights and forget the rest."

"What if we find something that is just a dollar or two more than our allowance? Is that okay?"

"No," Louise and I said in unison. Then one of us—I'd like to think it was Louise—said, "Unless you want to make up the difference with your own money."

"Can we use the money Grandma Plummer gives us for Christmas?"

"No. You have to pay in advance," I said. "No loans, no advances."

"That would be all right," Louise said. "At least they'd be spending her money on something they want."

"What if that isn't quite enough money? Can we work for the rest?"

I felt myself slipping into quicksand. This was how constitutions and bodies of law came about. This was how wars got started. We were on our way to a family constitution, judicial codex, and wars. I imagined layers of appellate courts with judges all looking like Louise. I was the prosecuting attorney. I, unlike Perry Mason, was never going to win.

As I lay awake that night, my mind slipped into its pseudo-philosophical mode. What's the point of giving if the receiver picks out the gift? What's a gift, anyway? What about gratitude? What about Jesus and the meaning of Christmas? My mind raced on as I went to sleep. By morning, I was filled with clichés and consternation, which I blurted out at Louise, who was still resting peacefully.

"This is a big mistake," I said through the dawn's early light. "We're making a big mistake. We should take that catalog and burn it."

"Look," she said without rolling toward me or opening her eyes. Her voice was dark and low. "We've already started this. If you want real trouble, just try to take it back. If you want to tell them we made a mistake and give them a boring lecture on the nature of giving and receiving, go ahead. But leave me out. We made a decision." Her deep breathing told me she had gone back to sleep in that instant. I was on my own.

My cowardice at facing the kids alone overrode my

reservations. They could always sense when I was acting on my own, when there was a disagreement between Louise and me, and that they could play off that weak spot, turn her against me, and get what they wanted. It's a gift they may have inherited from me, since I'd used the strategy many times against my own parents just to inflame a fight and relieve my own boredom.

My parents' weak spot, their Achilles' heel, was the garden. My father would come home from work, throw on bib overalls, and stride out into the yard. He always practiced walking and talking like he meant business, and he entered the yard the same way: shoulders back, brisk walk, a smile on his face. This spelled disaster for Mother's garden, which demanded love and care and delicate movements.

Being a teen with an adolescent agenda and code of ethics, I did everything I could to help him fall flat. One day I spotted him pruning a lilac bush that was overgrown with shoots and dead branches. He was trying to return it to its proper proportions and original beauty. The problem was that the more he cut away, the less it looked like a lilac bush and the more like a lone, dead pine tree.

Knowing this would drive my mother insane, I seized the

opportunity. "What are you doing with that bush?" I yelled at the top of my lungs. "My gosh, Mom's going to kill you when she sees that. It looks awful." I raised my voice a pitch to get Mother's attention from the house. "You've taken a beautiful bush and turned it into twisted twigs." I spit out the "t's" as hard as I could.

My dad, aware that I was setting him up, said, "Shut up, you stupid boy. You're going to have your mother on my neck." These words were more desperate than angry. My dad had a sense of humor, and even seeing it turned against himself had to strike him funny. About that time I saw my mother peeking through the back window to see what the ruckus was all about.

"Mom, come here and look what he's done. He just ruined this lilac bush."

Realizing now that he had done some damage, she came running out of the house. "Gail, I told you not to cut very much off that bush. Look at this," she said, pointing to the pile of limbs cut away.

"Elva," he said in a quivering, defensive tone (Mom was the only person I ever saw who could put Dad on the defensive), "you have to trim out that rubbish or the bush never stays healthy."

His voice had shifted toward whimpering. I moved in for the kill. "It just makes me sick," I said. "Here we had a beautiful bush that hid the waterfall, made it a surprise for people when they came around the corner, and now look. You've just turned one of the prettiest spots in the yard into twigs. It just makes me sick, heartsick," I said, borrowing language from my mother's vocabulary, things I would never say myself. She missed the irony.

"It makes me sick too," she said. "You've just ruined this beautiful part of the yard."

"I'll say. Poor white trash. That's what we are. It'll take years to recover. How long does it take a bush like this to grow back, Mom?"

Turning to Mother, Dad said, "Are you just going to stand here and allow this silly boy to sic you on me?"

He was desperate now, flailing hopelessly against the riptide. "You can call me silly if you want," I said, "but this is no silly matter. You've destroyed this bush and it makes me sick."

And so it went. And so it would now go for me if I tried to dump the catalog plan. Every generation knows how to drive the wedge between their parents. This is not acquired knowledge. It's instinctive, natural skill, and it's always driven by the law of the jungle.

I went to the kitchen to fix myself a cup of hot milk. Hot milk soothes me. Quiets me down. Gives me a warm feeling in the tummy. I usually save it for bedtime. I needed it now. Ed and Charles were sitting on the sofa when I entered the kitchen. They were poring over the catalog.

"Cool," Ed said. "That's really cool."

"But that's ten dollars too much," Charles said.

"But that's what I really want."

"Yeah, it's cool all right."

"I wish we had a little more money to spend."

I broke into a sweat. This had *ugly ending* written all over it. The beeper on the microwave sounded; I took my cup of milk and retreated to the bedroom. I was in way over my head this year. Where was Santa when I really needed him?

Christmas came and Christmas went. Tallying up the bills, I realized we had spent about a third more than we had planned and than we would have spent without the catalogs to help us. But the boys were happy for the first time in years. Not grateful, but happy. "We should do this every year," they said.

But when the catalogs began coming out for birthdays,

Easter, and boys' day (a Japanese holiday we mistakenly adopted for a short time thanks to a generous and well-meaning friend who brought them gifts one year), when they began to ask if they got the same gift allowance for those occasions as for Christmas, when the entire process shifted from the gift to its price tag, we tossed the catalog. Maybe we burned it in a ritual fire dance. I don't remember.

"Where's the LaBelle's catalog?" they asked one October.

"We trashed it," Louise and I said in unison.

"How come? How are we going to pick out our presents?" The tone was angry, desperate.

"We've decided to leave that up to Santa," I said.

"Uh-uhhhh. There ain't no Santa."

"Oh, yes, there is a Santa Claus, and he doesn't use catalogs. He knows just what's best for you. And that's what you'll get."

Dear Santa,

I am in college, and I would like a new alarm clock for Christmas. And a two-pound bag of peanut butter M&M's.

The alarm clock I now have doesn't seem to work very well. It keeps accurate time with its big red digits, and it beeps when (early) and how (intolerably) it is supposed to—but it doesn't wake me up.

At first I thought something was wrong with me. Its beeping aroused my consciousness only enough for me to reach across the bed and feel around until my fingers found the snooze button. This response became automatic, and it was happening five or six times each morning. I decided to move the bed 180 degrees, placing the pillow where my feet would normally be. Then the alarm clock was just out of reflex's reach.

It wasn't long before the sit-up/snooze-hit became a natural, flowing maneuver included in my semiconscious repertoire. Desperate for a solution, I again moved the bed, this time against the opposite wall. Surely, I hypothesized, the act of climbing all the way out of bed, wading through unlaundered clothes while stubbing my toes on books, a backpack, and a bike—just to arrive at the off button before the beeping completely ruined my well-rested mood—would be enough to wake me up so I could choose against the snooze option. My hypothesis proved inaccurate.

One night, I built a two-foot tower of books and dishes on top of the alarm clock. When I awoke, I quickly unstacked them and pressed snooze.

The next idea involved removing the actual snooze button, but the morning after doing so I shoved two fingers in the leftover hole and wiggled them around among the wires and circuit boards until the beeping stopped. Now there is duct tape covering that hole, and I am very fast at resetting the alarm with the remaining buttons, ten minutes at a time.

And I am desperate to wake up! I wish I could jump out of bed and straight into the shower. I want to shave, pray, and read the newspaper before facing the world. I dream of leaving the house with matching socks. But my alarm clock isn't waking me up.

Please, this Christmas I would like an alarm clock that works. And a two-pound bag of peanut butter M&M's.

> Sincerely,
> Matt, age 22

Dear Santa,

I don't know if I remembered to thank you for the fabulous trip to Africa you gave me last year. I had a wonderful time, and you are so thoughtful.

This year I shall be an armchair traveler. My Christmas wish will require some thought but will not be nearly as expensive.

Will you please deliver, on the 1st and 14th of every month, a new book? It can be a novel, biography, or cookbook (no self-help books, please). You know what I like. It's twenty-four books in all, but they can be paperback.

If you could bring with the book a pint of Ben and Jerry's Pfish Food ice cream, I should indeed have a blissful year.

> Thank you, dear Santa. You're a saint.
> Anne, age 57

Cyber Santa

Santa Claus has come to cyberspace. Browsing the Internet, I found 953,025 entries using the keywords *Santa Claus*. It's all there: the origins of Christmas candles, mistletoe, evergreens, bells, stockings, and Santa himself: pictures of Santa from the Middle Ages; Santa munching Cap'n Crunch Christmas Crunch; Santa reading *Emmet Otter's Jug Band Christmas*; Santa holding Barbie; and Santa selling "Santa one-dollar bills" in a "handsome engraved gift envelope" for just $4.95.

There are pictures of Santa having a snowball fight with an elf and favorite recipes from Mrs. Santa's kitchen: "'Twas the Night Before Bread Pudding," "Frog Bowl Full of Jelly," "Give Me Mores," and "Not Even a Mouse Salad." My mother would have jumped on a chair with her skirt pulled up at even the mention of that salad. I saw her jump on a bed and scream her head off in London once when a mouse appeared in our hotel room. It took one look at her and leaped into the heating vent.

There are interviews with Santa: "How many Santas are there, Mr. Claus?" "Where does Santa live?" "What are the names of the flying reindeer?" "Mr. Claus, are you real?" I would ask other questions: Have you had any hard times in your marriage, times when you thought you just might not make it? Any thoughts on diet and weight control? Is it true that you found the elves under mushrooms in Ireland?

And there are cyber-lists: "Top 10 Ways to Make the Nice List" ("Share the TV remote." "Clean the lint out of the dryer screen for the next person"); and "Top 10 Ways to Make the Naughty List" ("Put out milk for Santa Claus that's seven days beyond the expiration date").

But I would have given my right arm and left pinkie years ago to have had the "E-Mail X-Press" that I found. It allows kids to send an E-mail to Santa and get a response. I sat looking wistfully at the site and recalling the trillion hours I had spent as a father in Santa lines only to have one of my sons—whoever was youngest at the time—arch his back and scream at 130 decibels when I put him on Santa's lap. I could have saved myself the trauma. "Here, son. You don't need to visit Santa at the mall this year. Dad will help you write him a letter on the computer and he will answer you. We can even find a picture of him talking to you and saying, 'Ho, ho, ho.' What do you mean, Santa's not in the computer? He's everywhere, son. PC. Macintosh. He's a Microsoft program. It doesn't make any difference. Just give it a try. C'mon."

I know E-mail's not the same as a personal visit. But neither does E-mail cause post-traumatic stress syndrome the way sitting on Santa's lap can. Just to see if E-mail is as satisfying as the real thing, I wrote Santa an E-mail:

"Dear Santa. My name is Tommy. I want a puppy for Christmas. My mom says I should get one at the animal shelter. She says there are already too many dogs in the world. But I want a french poodle and the animal shelter doesn't have any french poodles. Do you have a french poodle that you could bring me for Christmas?"

I used my childhood moniker and erased a few dead giveaways that I was not a little kid (capital "f" on *French*, a comma between *poodle* and *and*)—the kind of thing a sharp-eyed, otherwise unemployed Ph.D. in English would spot as he prepared to e-mail me back. Then I selected a stamp from the several shown on the site—one of Rudolph, batty eyed, just the way I imagine him—and, voilà, my completed envelope popped onto the screen. In the upper left corner was "Tommy," and the envelope was addressed "To: Santa, the North Pole" (in a funky colored font with a Santa hat on the "S"). Did Santa reply? Not yet. I sent the E-mail in July. I'm looking forward to his letter when he gets back to his computer.

There were other sites that I couldn't get to work. One was a "Santa karaoke" that was supposed to play Christmas songs with all the fidelity my laptop computer could muster. It played one measure before it broke down and I had to restart the computer. Another site resulted in a message on my screen: "This site has been blocked at your request." I don't remember requesting such a block, but I suspect it was something very naughty and inappropriate for Santa to be involved with.

Now, I could be cynical and nasty and say all this Santa stuff is just raw commercialism. People trying to make a fast buck off an old guy who had to move to the frozen north to escape the IRS, who's too tired to lift a razor to his beard, and whose best friends were found behind mushroom stalks. People trying to get rich off other people's sentimentality. I expected that. Every corporation from Coca Cola to Pepsi, Norelco to Budweiser, and Sega to Seagrams is bullish on Santa Claus. Is there a Santa Claus? Corporate America answers with a resounding "YES."

On the other hand, some web sites are created by people who just want to be Santa Claus, take time to answer a little kid's E-mail, send out some free recipes, write up interviews. People just trying to be nice. They have gone to the trouble of hiring an artist and a computer specialist to design a site, and then they pay twenty or thirty or more dollars a month to keep it going. Yes, they have altered the image of Santa a bit, added twists—some grotesque—to an already well-worked-over legend. But that's what we do with legends—Abe Lincoln, Butch Cassidy, St. Nicholas. We take a snippet of history and decorate it. The raw material becomes as ornamented as a Christmas tree.

Yes, Santa's gone cyber. He'll never be the same again. And that's human necessity. We can no more do without Santa than we can do without chocolate. But we can't take him as he once was, either. It's a new day, and with it comes a new Santa—a Santa who was once a shaman but now communicates on a computer; a Santa whom you could once touch in a mall, but who now has a booth in a microchip; a Santa who remains, in some evolving form, Father Christmas.

Dear Santa,

I am writing to you this year from 30,000 feet in the air as I fly over the American Southwest; a trip you have made many times, though perhaps at lower altitudes. (By the way, I have always wondered how high reindeer can fly without suffering nosebleeds. Any idea?) And of course I am writing this letter on the latest supercharged laptop computer and regretting that I don't have your e-mail address so that you could receive this instantly.

Things have changed a lot since I first wrote you painstaking letters in longhand as a child, and not all of it has been for the better.

And this brings me right to the point. What I want for Christmas this year is less, not more! I am wondering if we couldn't slightly alter the so-called "KISS" business principle (Keep it Simple, Stupid) to Keep it Simple, Santa. For starters, I don't want to see your picture in the store or hear by song that you are coming to town until Thanksgiving is over, please. As it is now, I have to push my way through the Christmas ornaments to get to the Halloween stuff at WalMart. And I would like less paper in my life, too, please. I feel nothing but compassion for the poor postal worker who must heft all those "Early Holiday" catalogs around to our doorstep beginning the middle of August. (No wonder they sometimes go ballistic!) And I would like fewer holiday parties to attend or prepare for, a greatly reduced number of boughs that I must deck my halls with, and about half the number of fruitcakes I receive from well-meaning friends. On second thought, scratch the fruitcakes altogether!

Now, I know what you must be thinking: This man is a Bah Humbug! I am really not a Bah Humbug. Underneath it all, no one likes Christmas more than I do, Santa, and no one more enjoys all the musical and decorative bits and pieces that go with it. But, to paraphrase Wordsworth: "Christmas is too much with us late and soon, Getting and spending we lay waste our powers, Little in Christmas we see that is ours." So what I want for Christmas is the Christmas I remember from my growing years when I used to write you in longhand. A simpler Christmas that lasted just long enough and didn't stick around forever like unwanted house guests. And please remind me that decking the halls is not a contest. Remind me that it really *is* the thought that counts. And most of all, please remind me that peace on earth and good-will to all people is the best present we could all give and receive.

Thanks in advance, Santa, and, if you have any questions about any of this, you can reach me by E-mail, voice mail, or fax, or of course you can call me at the office number, the home number, the cell phone in the car, or my mobile number, or you can simply have me paged.

Yours for a more simple Christmas,
Gordon, age 52

Dear Santa,

You probably don't remember me, as it has been more years than I care to think about since I wrote you last. It might jog your memory to know that my letters came from a little town in Canada, and I probably asked for every toy in the Montgomery Ward catalog.

The reason I haven't written in all these years is because I really have just about all I could ask for, and could never think of one more thing that would make my life more complete—that is, until now. I lost something this summer that I'm hoping you can replace, because you always did come up with just what I wanted.

I seem to have lost part of my health! Not all of it, you understand—just a knee, a back, and sometimes, I think, a part of my brain. I know it is a lot to ask, but, you see, I love to hike and ski and bike and visit with good friends, and I really miss that part of my life.

You've probably never had a request like this before, so I will understand if you've just run out of "good health" items this year. That really is all I want for Christmas, though, so do your best!

> Your old friend,
> Dorothy, age 66

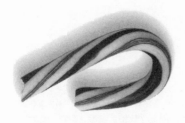

From Scrooge to Santa and Back Again

I find that when I'm not wearing a Santa suit, I'm a Scrooge. The spirit of generosity has flown back to wherever it came from, and a closefisted, grudging, let-'em-earn-their-keep attitude has again taken possession of my mind and body.

For instance, I walk into my office to pull materials together for a final exam that I am giving at 11:00. The phone is ringing. The caller ID says it is from home. "Hi," I say.

"Hi," Louise says.

"I'm glad you called," I say. "I was listening to 'Car Talk' on the radio on the way down. The Click and Clack brothers say the title of their new CD is 'Men Are from GM, Women Are from Ford, and Lawyers are from Chrysler.'" We laugh.

Louise changes the tone. "Sam wants to know if he can have $100 for Christmas presents," she says. I can hear Sam bleating in the background.

This always makes me crazy. Sam has had a job. Sam has earned money. Sam has spent his money. Now Sam wants my money. It is also a trap. If I say no, I am saying he'll have to embarrass himself, because the gifts are for members of his choral group, his girlfriend, his friends at church, yadda, yadda, yadda.

"What's he going to do to earn the money if we give it to him?" I ask.

Louise repeats my question to Sam.

More bleating. "C'mon," I hear him say. "I take care of a lot of things around here."

Maybe. He put up Christmas lights, changed the oil in the car, shoveled the walks. Of course, I'll have to take down the Christmas lights and pay for the oil change. I'm huffing and puffing now.

"You know this always sets me off," I say to Louise.

"You're always surprised, aren't you?"

"Yeah," I say. "Aren't you?"

"No, I expect it," she says.

"Well, you take care of it," I say. "I can't deal with it."

The subject changes. "The East High people called," Louise says. "They want our names, addresses, and other information for a directory of alumni that they want to sell for $60."

In the background I hear Sam say, "That's a waste of money."

Now, this sears my already tender sensitivities. "Wait a minute," I say to Louise. "That is none of his business. He hits us up for $100. Then, when we consider spending money on ourselves, he has opinions."

Louise laughs and says to Sam, "Dad says to mind your own business."

I hear him muttering something to Louise.

"He says we should be spending our money on West High." West High is his school.

"We are," I say. "I'm just about to donate $100 to Christmas presents for the West High chorale."

Louise turns to Sam. "We went to East High. If we want to give money to East High, we will."

What's mine is mine and what's yours is mine. That's what adolescents think.

This became abundantly clear the other day when Louise and I were away. Again it was our eighteen-year-old Sam, the good son, the faithful son, the sinless son, who cut class with a buddy, came home, got the keys to the convertible, put down the top, and went joyriding. The responsible, even-keeled Sam embraced the reckless, manic spirit of Ferris Bueller.

I might not have been so peeved if I hadn't expressly forbidden his use of the convertible. I had taken him to lunch the day before and told him that Louise and I would be driving 150 miles south that day because she was giving a talk in a distant town to a group of obedient young people and their parents.

"We may stay overnight in a motel," I said, "or we may drive home."

"Why?" he asked.

"Why what?" I asked.

"Why come home?"

"Well, I just didn't want to leave you alone," I said.

"Don't worry about me," he said.

"You'll take care of the dog and the parrot?" I asked.

"We'll be fine," he said. His voice was calm, reassuring. "I do it all the time."

In a moment of doubt, of distrust—I cannot account for the reason except that a dark feeling prompted me—I said, "Don't take the convertible to school."

He blinked. "Why not?" he asked.

"Because bad things happen to nice cars in your school parking lot," I said.

"Like what?"

Sam was now in serious denial. Early in the year he had written an angry essay for the school paper blaming the administrators for failing to police the parking lots properly. He cited several incidents of car vandalism, including keyed paint and slashed convertible roofs.

"You know darn well what, Sam," I said. "You're the one telling stories about broken windows and slashed tires. Don't take the convertible while we're gone. Don't take it to school. Don't drive it. Period."

He muttered. In retrospect, I realize, he offered no assurance that he would obey.

We called him that night from the motel. "We'll be home

tomorrow afternoon," Louise told him. "I have to stop at my office, and then we'll be home."

"What time will that be?" he wanted to know.

"Oh, don't expect us before late afternoon," Louise said.

"Dad too?" he asked.

"Yes," she said.

As often happens in strange beds in strange places with strange mosquitoes, we didn't sleep well. Although we had been exhausted the night before, although we slept in separate beds to maximize our chances for a comfortable and conflict-free sleep, we awoke around five. We tossed and turned for long minutes to get more sleep, but we were both wide awake.

"Let's get out of here," I said. "We can go straight home and finish sleeping in a familiar bed."

Driving even at a leisurely pace, we pulled up to the house around 10:00 A.M. and found the Geo Prizm—the car Sam drives with 170,000 miles on the odometer, the car with dents and bumps all over it, the car of little interest to vandals because the damage has already been done—sitting in front of the house. The Miata was gone.

Louise has always accused me of overreacting. It's a mercy-justice dichotomy in our marriage. I paraded my wrath in all its glory before her. "The little jerk," I hollered. "He betrayed me. He'll never drive again." I raged on, threatening various forms of capital punishment from drawing and quartering to burning at the stake to parboiling his head.

When I had run out of threats, Louise said calmly, "I'm glad he's finally showing some spunk."

"Huh?" I said.

"I'm glad he's finally had the guts to break a rule," she said. "He's always been such a goody-goody."

"You've got to be kidding," I said. "He's just rebelled against a very specific rule I laid down, and you're saying you're glad he had the courage to break it. I told him not to take the car to school. I didn't stammer around. I didn't qualify that. I told him under no circumstances to take the car, and you're saying you're glad. Have I got that right?"

"Well, partly," she said. "What he did was wrong, but it's time he showed some guts."

Realizing I had only a partial ally, not to say alien, and realizing after thirty-three years of marriage that making and enforcing rules on my own never works, I took a deep breath and assumed a more diplomatic tone. "I still think he has to have some consequences for this. So what do you propose?"

"He can't drive anything but the Geo for a month," she said.

That worked for a time. But after he'd been accepted to a fine university and realized that his adoring parents would put up with a whole lot more malarkey now that he'd shown how dazzling he could be, he upped the ante. Just a few days before he left for college, Sam sensed that Louise had redefined the empty nest syndrome. It didn't mean missing the children. It meant living alone with me. Knowing this, Sam knew he had more power with Louise than I did. He asked her if he could use the Miata for a date. She agreed. We went out with friends in their car. When we returned, there was a note pinned to the door. →

The Jeep was my car. The Miata was Louise's car. He took my car. Having negotiated with Louise for the Miata, he took my car. I stormed around the house to no avail.

"He's going in three weeks. Just be kind. In five years, he'll be grown up and

I Took The Jeep. In Trade for Miata Please love me I'm leaving in 3 weeks
Sam

you'll see a whole new man," Louise said. Something about the lilt of her voice—soothing, calming, sensing how crazed I was, like a wolf with its foot in a trap—quieted me down.

The next night we went out in the Jeep and returned to find Sam's car sitting where the Miata had been. Another note was pinned to the door →

"That's it," Louise raged. "It's one thing when he takes your car without permission. It's quite another when he takes mine."

> I went out with the miata at 7:30 PM with Emily and friends. Considering that your love for me is so strong and there is only 23 days left. Sam

"I'm sure you'll know just what to say to him," I said.

The conversation took place the next morning in the TV room. I was in the kitchen fixing some hot chocolate.

"Sam," Louise said in a firm, level voice that she reserves for momentous occasions, "you took my car last night. Don't ever do that again without asking."

"Sorry, Mom," I heard Sam say. His tone was submissive.

"One note—that's cute," Louise said. "Two notes—that's too much." And she stepped out of the TV room with a no-nonsense motion that Sam knew could not be challenged.

"Hot chocolate?" I asked as she whisked into the kitchen. "It's an aphrodisiac."

"No, thanks," she said. "On second thought, yes. I'd like a cup."

It's a good thing I put on a Santa suit once a year, or my sons would all be dead. Sometimes I wonder if Santa would be a tough disciplinarian. Would he ground his kids? Would he take away their driver's licenses if they went out for an unauthorized spin in the sleigh, pushing to see just how fast those reindeer really could fly? Or would he be more like a grandfather, just smiling or laughing when the kids did something naughty? Would he get the same satisfaction that I get watching my sons try to cultivate their own kids and remembering how I tried in vain to turn them into responsible adults? Maybe there's some great pleasure, which I'm just beginning to sense when I'm wearing my Santa suit or my grandfather hat, a pleasure that I just can't know when I'm rearing my kids, because I miss the Santa perspective. I can't see how it all turns out.

Dear Santa,

I'm sure you have your reasons for not always bringing what's requested. Remember the five consecutive years I asked for a puppy? Remember the pages and pages of pleading and all the reasons I gave for really *needing* a puppy? And I didn't put anything else on my list for fear that you would accidentally choose something other than the puppy. Remember? The first year you gave me a sewing kit. Yippee. The other years are just one big, package-opening blur.

Now I have an idea I hope you will consider. Most people have too many things anyway. And the "somethin' for nuthin'" attitude continues year after year. So, my suggestion: make people work for what they want. Every year, you bring an assignment. If the assignment is completed by the following Christmas, then you leave a gift. For example, my neighbor, Captain Blockwatch. You could ask him to, oh, I don't know . . . mow my lawn all summer. I would be more than happy to report on his progress as *my* assignment. I've got other neighbors, friends, and family |members who would really benefit from thinking of others for a change. They could bring meals and tend my children, and there is always plenty of laundry and housework. I'd be glad to send you more ideas if you need them.

If you decide to disregard this and to continue as always, I would like you to notice that I am sending my request indisputably early. I would really, *really* like a new computer this year. You know, one that would bring me into the twentieth century just in time for the twenty-first. Please include a big-screen color monitor and a fancy printer.

Sincerely,
Kathryn, age 34

I'm Santa, I Light Up the Room

When I'm in my everyday clothes, people see me and think, "There's Tom Plummer"—if they think anything at all. Strangers pass me by without looking into my Frank-Sinatra-blue eyes or staring at my Cary-Grant dimples or turning around to follow my Arnold-Schwarzenegger body. I once had a friend who was so good-looking that girls would follow him down the street. That has never happened to me. No one ever follows me. Not down the street. Not into my office. Not into the men's room.

Not since first grade, when a couple of girls stalked me. I was walking home from Douglas School one day when Molly

Zanuck came out from behind some euonymus bushes and said she was going to kiss me. She had her lips puckered into a big bloom, arms extended. I sprinted out of there.

And Hildegard Hildesheimer got up and announced in first-grade Show and Tell that she hadn't told anyone yet, but she loved Tommy Plummer. Hildegard, for some medical reason I-know-not-what, was always breaking her arms and legs. This aroused my morbid curiosity but absolutely no passion. My self-esteem was barely above the toilet bowl, and being stalked by a girl with hyperactive lips or one with frail bones was a circuit overload.

After I got glasses in second grade, I looked like a hoot owl, and no one bothered me much anymore. Some teachers liked the horn-rimmed look, I suppose because they thought—hoped, maybe—there were some brains behind it. I've never figured out the connection between myopia and brains in a teacher's mind. To most other folks, it's a nerdy look. Eyes magnified three times—even Frank-Sinatra-blue eyes—don't say *smart* to them. They say *blowfish.*

Eventually, as an adult, this cost me part-time work. At least, I blame it on the look. When Louise and I were desperate for extra cash once, I applied to a business consulting firm for a job as one of those guys who goes out to corporations whose executives have burned their brains out with work overloads. This consultant—that would be me—gets them all fired up about their navels and convinces them they could sell Royal Copenhagen china to Attila the Hun if they could just get their attitudes overhauled. I had a couple of colleagues—professor types—who were doing this and making a fair bit of money on the side. I considered myself at least as attractive as they were. Both of them had less hair.

I sent the consulting firm my résumé, and in a few days a guy called who said he had been a college teacher and was now making megabucks as the senior vice president of this company. I could make megabucks too, he implied. "I think we've got a match," he said. That meant, I inferred, that my credentials—academic degrees and life as a German professor—somehow added up to make me a potentially competent cheerleader for corporate America.

I was to make a ten-minute presentation to some of the company executives, he said, on how to do something—the topic was up to me. I stewed for some time about the topic because, to be honest, I had not the slightest idea what executives needed to learn. I finally settled on teaching them how to keep a journal by rush-writing. I could do that in five to ten minutes. We would hear what they'd written in a short time and, I imagined, have a few laughs.

On the appointed day I put on a starched white dress shirt, a gray flannel suit, a new tie (hand selected by Louise), and shined black shoes, and drove the sixty or so miles to the headquarters of the consulting firm. I was ushered into a meeting room with a long table, and company executives, some looking quite bored and frumpy, soon filed in.

After a cursory introduction, I began my presentation. It was the kind of moment I'd had many times before in teaching German 101, a required course for university graduation. The captive students resented the requirement and hated me for executing the university's demands. They couldn't care less that I was just the messenger. And now it was *déjà vu*. I began telling these bored-looking, captive executives about rush-writing, and I had the feeling of being up to my waist in mud with a tiger bearing down. I was going to die.

In a short interview after the presentation, the CEO said he was sure I was a fine college teacher, he'd be happy if any of his children could take a course from me, but, frankly, and these are his exact words, "You don't light up the room." And the former-college-teacher-turned-senior-vice-president added, "Your topic suggested you really didn't know much about your audience."

"But," the CEO said, "I hear your wife does a lot of public speaking. Would she be interested?"

"Nope," I said. "She's too busy." I really wanted to say, "Drop dead."

But when I'm Santa Claus, all of my dullness dissipates. The glasses turn into required costume. I light up the room. I light up the universe. I should've gone in my Santa outfit for that interview. I should've begun wearing Santa suits in third grade. Girls would've followed me down the street. At preference dances girls would have introduced me to their friends: "Hi, I'd like you to meet my date, Santa Claus."

When I'm in my Santa suit, my karma is cooking. I can feel it warming up by the end of November. Before Christmas Eve arrives, I go to Salt Lake Costume and rent their $55 Santa outfit (the good one, which I've reserved well in advance), dig out my black, spit-shined army combat boots (which are better than wearing black shoes under those silly-looking fake boots), get several pillows to amplify my 160-pound frame (someone once told me my butt was too skinny for Santa Claus), and buy several pounds of candy kisses wrapped in red and green foil.

Around six o'clock I get dressed. I strap on the padded vest that comes with the costume, hitch pillows to my inferior derriere with bungee cords, don pants and jacket, have Louise lace and tie my boots, which I can no longer reach, put on the beard and wig, and slip on the white gloves. *Voilà*–no more nerd. I light up the room. I dump the bags of kisses into my Santa sack and toddle off to the car. After a brief struggle to get behind the wheel, I drive away yelling, "On Dancer, on Prancer."

I waddle to the first door, adjusting the bungee cord, and ring the bell. A little kid answers. And screams. Yes, screams. "It's Santa Claus. Mommy, Daddy, Santa Claus is here." And a half dozen other kids come running and the parents behind them, and they're all jumping around and hollering and hugging me. Except the baby, who thinks Count Dracula has come, and starts wailing. And everybody laughs. The family interrupts whatever they're doing because the fat elf in red has arrived with goodies.

They usher me into the living room and have me sit down, which I do as best I can to accommodate the padding. And the mom yells at the dad, "Where's the camera? Get the camera. Who's got the video camera?" And there's a brief skirmish as they blame each other for misplacing the camera or not having bought film. But it's Christmas, it's time to be jolly, so the fight is short. Eventually, after crashing through drawers and cabinets, they find more film. "Hold on, Santa, hold on," they yell.

"I'm fine," I say, "I'm just fine." And I really am, in spite of the scratchy beard and the bungee cord crawling into uncomfortable places. This is the best moment of the year. The little kids are trying to climb into my lap, and the older ones are pushing and shoving for position.

And finally the parents are ready with the point-and-shoot and the video camera, and the first little kid climbs onto my lap. "Would you like a kiss from Santa?" I ask.

She shakes her head because the beard really isn't something she wants to kiss. But she has misunderstood. I hand her a few chocolate kisses. "What would you like Santa to bring you for Christmas?" I ask. This is a little sadistic pleasure for me, because it is now Christmas Eve, and I know good and well that the parents have no time to change presents or buy more. The stores are closed. And they squirm a bit while little Jenny screws up her eyes and thinks.

"A Barbie doll," she says.

There's a look of relief in the parents' eyes, suggesting they haven't messed up yet.

"What else?" I ask. The parents shift from foot to foot. Jenny puts her finger to her lips, rolls her eyes, and thinks some more. "A bike," she says. Again the parents look relieved.

I don't push the game too far because, after all, it's Christmas, and it's not nice to torture parents on Christmas. When the kids and adults have all sat on my lap and the photos are taken, and I'm seeing spots from the flashing cameras, I say, "Well, it's time to be off. I've got to be in Russia in an hour, and I still have to pack my sleigh." And the parents laugh, and the kids look amazed, and I adjust my straps and toddle out midst screams of "Merry Christmas, Santa."

"Merry Christmas to all," I holler. "Merry Christmas to all."

I wish I knew where those executives lived. I'd take them some kisses and hug their family and show them how I can light up the room. They'd yell and holler along with their kids, and that would be a good moment for all of us.

Dear Santa,

For so many years as a child I wrote letters to you asking for dolls whose eyes open when they sit up and close when they lie down, and for so many years you brought me perfect gifts, gifts I have always treasured.

I know your time is valuable and your efforts are directed to the wants and needs of children, but I must ask one more present of you, if you feel I am deserving of such a gift. You see, I married a man who is a doll, one whose eyes are open when he is sitting up, but whose eyes close when he lies down. Just as I open, say, a socio-economic or domestic discourse, he falls off to sleep. With the dousing of the lights he nods off, while I turn into a Chatty Kathy with a perpetually taut pull cord. This is annoying to my husband, who sees the bedroom as many things, none of them a forum for social, political, economic, or religious discussion.

I am not asking for a new spouse, but perhaps for a slight alteration in his model's specifications. Magic being your hallmark, you could, I am hoping, reprogram him with an inclination toward conversation until, say, eleven o'clock at night, couldn't you? All aspects of our marriage would improve with such a change; he wouldn't have to hear me complain about his reticence, and I would find greater appreciation for his attention. I hope I have been a good enough person this year for you to consider my supplication, as I have worked cheerfully wiping both ends of my children, maintaining my share of the housework, and never criticizing my doll of a spouse to anyone at all. Okay, maybe just once or twice.

Thank you for all of the joy your gifts have brought me throughout my life, Santa. If you choose not to bestow the gift for which I am asking, I promise to still believe in you.

Sincerely,
Jill, age 28

Dear Santa Claus and Mrs. Santa Claus (I don't know your name):

Thank you. Thank you. Thank you for the cymbals. I played them in the Fourth of July neighborhood parade.

One day driving down the road worrying, I suddenly thought, "I've got cymbals."

As you know, I've never written a letter to you before, certainly never a wish list. I like you as you are and have been to me. I like your causing me to kick my feet above the bed like an airborne wheel half Christmas Eve night because I couldn't sleep waiting for morning when I was five, though I'd asked for nothing. I like your showing up twice unexpectedly on Christmas Eve so that our meal was more festive than I could have planned. I like your noticing that I have yearned for fifty-five years for rhythm-band cymbals and giving me a pair of twenty-inch Zildjian concert cymbals that I would never have dreamed of asking for. I like your making my mother cry fifty years ago by giving her a set of hand-painted English bone china to make her table pretty when she put all her hard work on it for guests to enjoy eating. I like your giving me a garnet ring when I thought I was still a child but you noticed I had become an adult and the ring told me so. Your unexpected, unearned gifts tell me you know me. I'm loved.

There are echoes: from the time my daughter was just beginning to baby-sit. One day when we were shopping for school clothes miles from home, I saw a red print robe, said, "I like it," and moved on. Christmas morning months later, I was surprised to see a big box from this barely-eleven-year-old daughter in department store wrapping. It was the red robe. She had saved her baby-sitting money, told me one day she was going to play with a neighbor friend, but actually walked a mile and a half to catch a bus to the store, put the robe on layaway, walked/bused home, walked/bused again after saving minuscule baby-sitting earnings and allowance for months, bought the robe, had it wrapped, and watched my face Christmas morning. She knows you. So do my sons. So does my husband, who woke me up at 1:30 A.M. on our limited-income-first-Christmas because he couldn't wait for me to open his gift to me. He had filled a small matchbox with rice and tied on a buckeye picked off the grass, beautifully wrapped the mysterious-sounding, strange shape, and put it under the tree for me to shake and smell, guess at, and be surprised with. Surprise, I thought, was a wonderful gift. But there was more: a pair of comfortable, beautiful Italian shoes I had thought we could scarcely afford and an umbrella for my two-mile walks to school every day.

Santa, I don't think you are a pagan relic, or a greedy gourmand breaking out of a red jacket, or an advertiser, or a judge hiding behind a white beard. Thank you for the cymbals.

Francine, age 63

Geeks Bearing Gifts

My stinginess is legendary in the family, as my sons' testimonials at family gatherings will attest. I am, as a friend said, the great "naysayer." Whenever sons as teenagers asked to borrow the family car (for many of their growing-up years we had just one car), my stomach would tighten and my pulse quicken. "No," I'd say, "you can't use the car tonight."

"Why not?"

"Because it's my car, that's why."

"Are you and Mom going somewhere tonight?"

"We might. It doesn't matter."

In less time than it takes a baby to soil a clean diaper, we'd be at each other's throats.

If Louise was anywhere near, she'd jump into the fray, give

the whimpering kid the keys to the car, and tell me I couldn't control the car that way. "They are teenagers, for heaven's sake," she'd say. "You can't just keep them trapped at home. Driving is half the fun of being a teenager."

And although this rationale made eminently good sense to me, I hated it on a visceral level. I'd spend the night obsessing about what would happen if they had an accident (they all had at least one), what would happen to our insurance rates, which we could barely afford with teenage sons, what we would do while the car was in a repair shop, yadda yadda yadda.

Our son Ed scared me the most, and so I was most reluctant to loan him the car. Before he got his license, I would go out driving with him in our stick-shift Toyota Tercel. Each time I swore to myself that I'd keep my cool, and each time I lost it. Usually when he turned right from the left lane in front of a speeding car. I'd yell and curse and make him feel like a no-good kid, which I felt terrible about, but I just couldn't quit yelling in the face of imminent death.

While he was learning to drive, Louise went with him once. They were gone about ten minutes. I heard the car turn into the driveway and squeal to a stop. Doors slammed, and Louise stormed into the house yelling, "I will not go out with him ever again. I will not die this way."

One night the police called and said a woman had just complained that she had nearly been killed in an intersection by a car bearing our license plate, 001 ASK. (This was not a vanity plate—it was just luck of the draw and unfortunate for anyone wanting to remain anonymous.) Ed had been out in the car. The woman was, it seems, proceeding through a green light when this "little red car" ran its red light, whizzed in front of her, and left her sitting in a cold sweat. The other driver, she said, made an obscene gesture at her when he passed in front of her bumper. The first part of the story sounded exactly like Ed. The second part was hard to believe. I had never seen him make an obscene gesture in his life.

"She said he was going about seventy miles an hour," the policeman told me. "I assume you know how to handle this, since we didn't catch him."

"Yes, I do," I said. "Consider it taken care of."

Ed had told me he was going to a meeting for employees at Hardee's. I took a car that we were tending for Louise's parents and headed for Hardee's. "He did come in, but our meeting was canceled," a young woman behind the counter reported.

"He seemed upset. He said he was going to see the family doctor."

"At nine o'clock at night?"

"That's what he said." She shrugged.

"The doctor isn't in at this time of night," I said, and then realized I was talking to a totally uninterested party. "Thanks," I said.

I went home. By now, Ed, who had been badly shaken by the red-light incident himself, had returned. "Dad's out looking for you," his younger brother Charles had told him. "And he's mad. The police called."

Louise met me at the door. "Now, just calm down," she said. "He's scared out of his mind. Don't be too hard on him."

"I'd like to tear him apart," I said. "But I'll try to control myself." She followed me into his room. There was Ed, his six-foot-three frame curled into a fetal position on his bed. He looked pathetic, lying there waiting to be slaughtered.

I took a breath. "Ed," I said, in the softest, quietest, gentlest tone I could muster, "would you like to tell me what happened?"

Before he could answer, Louise, the usually cool one, broke in. "Are you on drugs? The policeman said you made an obscene gesture and the people at Hardee's said you were going to the doctor."

"I didn't make any gestures," Ed said. "When I thought she was going to hit me, I held up my hands, like this." He held up his hands, his long, bony fingers spread apart to show us. I could see how she could have mistaken that for an obscene gesture under the circumstances. "I told my boss I was going to the doctor because I was so shook up I couldn't think straight."

I kept my low pitch. "Ed, you nearly killed someone tonight. If you drive that way again, I'll have your license revoked." I said a few more stern words as calmly as I could.

"You were good," Louise said as we left his room. "You handled that just right."

"I don't want him to use the car ever again," I said. "I lied about having his license revoked later. I want it revoked now."

"Don't make threats you can't keep," Louise, who had recovered from her outburst, cautioned. "You know he'll use it again. He has to. Just take a deep breath and let it pass."

A week or two later I overheard Ed talking to Charles. "When Dad talks to me in that low, soft voice it makes my spine crawl. I wish he'd just yell."

This gave me some satisfaction, but, of course, it was the wrong kind. I hadn't eased his anxiety, I'd heightened it. I could have said any number of things, I suppose. "How can I help you, Ed?" "You must have scared yourself pretty badly." I had stopped short of that.

If I've given to my sons ungenerously, I've given to my wife manipulatively. In the early years of our marriage, when I'd done something stupid and Louise was so mad I was afraid she'd file for divorce, I'd buy her some flowers or a gift. Once, when I was especially worried, I bought her a crystal vase. This was not done with the sole intention of bringing her joy. It was done with the idea of getting myself off the hook. I wanted to think of it as a peace offering, but really it wasn't.

The ploy never worked as well as I hoped. Louise would receive the gift graciously enough, but she never hugged and kissed me and told me it was all right if I was a dork sometimes. She always seemed to know when my gestures were less than sincere—or, let's say, had an ulterior motive. In fact, she wrote about that very thing in one of her novels. Bjorn and his wife, Trish, have had a tiff. The doorbell rings. It is a delivery of a dozen roses to Trish from Bjorn, a peace offering. When Bjorn enters the room, we read:

Trish, having read the note [with the roses], swung on Bjorn, embracing him with her one free arm. "Of course I forgive you." She kissed his lips. "Bjorn, they're so beautiful." She kissed him again. "I've never had such a lovely gift. Thank you!" Kiss. Kiss. Kiss. Smooch. Smooch.

It is their friend Fleur who sees through the whole thing. Alone with Bjorn's sister Kate, she declares, "Roses don't solve anything. It's just a bribe to get her to be nice to him again. My mother fell for it all the time. Geez."

The giving thing is a problem I suppose I will never quite be rid of. A slightly ungenerous spirit. Just a bit off the mark. That's not to say that I don't ever deal with it. I do. Over the years I've learned to go against this dark side of my personality (actually I have many dark sides) and do something spontaneously generous, even if it frightens me, not to get something back, but just to make someone else happy. Still, I have this little nasty voice inside me that whispers, "You're a geek bearing gifts."

My innards constantly rebel against the notion that giving is just plain right, that, as Longfellow once wrote, "the greatest grace of a gift, perhaps, is that it anticipates and admits of no return" (*Journals and Letters,* 28 Feb. 1871). And, I might add, anticipates and admits of the possibility that you may actually be charged outrageously by your insurance company for the gift you give.

That's why I like the Santa I know. Unlike me, he's an absolutely generous giver, a giver without strings attached. Yes, I know about the legends of Santa leaving coal in the stockings of bad children. I've heard distraught parents hollering at their kids in the mall, "If you don't stop screaming right now, Santa's going to smack you when you sit on his knee." Yes, I sang the song with my grade-school compatriots at Christmastime:

> He knows if you've been bad or good,
> So be good for goodness' sake.

But I don't believe it. Whether the writer of the lyrics believed his own stuff or not, I don't believe in a Santa Claus who functions like George Orwell's Big Brother, operating monitors like lie detectors to read our every secret thought, our every spontaneously nasty deed, a Santa Claus who threatens to withhold gifts or even smack us around because he is a conditional giver. Yes, I know about the Dutch Swarte Piet who tags along with Sinter Klaas and throws bad children in his bag and swings them around. I just don't believe it.

I believe in a Santa Claus who rises above all my emotional junk and, unlike me, always gives unconditionally. If he's just like me, what's so hot about Santa Claus? That makes him as dangerous as I am on a bad day. I believe there's nothing dangerous about Santa Claus. That's what makes him Santa Claus. He gives chocolate kisses and presents, no questions asked, no conditions imposed.

Santa Claus is like our friends C. B. and B. B., who spontaneously wrote us a check one day for an enormous amount of money so we could buy a house we loved. No interest. No repayment date. Just a huge check. I didn't ask for the money. They just knew we wanted the house and said, out of the blue, "We want to help. Pay it back when you have the money." There were no strings attached, no hooks, just pure love and friendship.

That's Santa Claus. I'm not there yet. I want to be, but I'm not—not all the time.

But something magical happens when I put on my red suit and black boots and fake white hair and beard. Suddenly I'm generosity personified. I know what it must be like to be Santa Claus. I am Santa Claus. How does that happen? I put on the suit, and my personality changes.

Sometimes I become more aggressive. Once when I was driving between friends' houses, I saw another Santa Claus climbing out of his car. I screeched to a halt, jumped out, and yelled at him, "Get off the street, you fraud."

He was up to the challenge. "You get off the street, you fraud," he yelled back.

And as if responding to the downbeat of a conductor, we hollered in unison, "Merry Christmas!"

Dear Santa,

As I approach the autumn (all right, already—winter) of my life, my heart is softened, and I seek only for things of real importance and lasting value for me, my family, and indeed the world. Thus, for Christmas this year please bring:

Health
Satisfaction with current circumstances
Peace throughout the world
Shelter and sustenance for the needy
Relief for those who suffer
An F-16 and a year's supply of fuel
Renewed 20—20 vision to fly it safely.

Thanks,
Jimmy, age 57

To: Santa Claus
From: Annie, age 45
Re: Naughty and Nice—The Short List

After 45 years of carrying around the above referenced bag-
gage—my own personally maintained Naughty and Nice List—I
have decided that it is time to lighten my emotional, middle-
aged load and reduce the list to a more manageable size. I've
made the list; now would you check it twice?

	Naughty	Nice
1950s	Nikita Khrushchev	Dad and Mom
	Joseph McCarthy	Older brother
	Boy next door	2nd grade teacher
	Accordion salesmen	Captain Kangaroo
1960s	Mom	Dad
	Fidel Castro	Older brother
	Everybody in junior high	Younger brother
	Ho Chi Minh	Grandpa and Grandma
	KKK	The Beatles
1970s	Dad and Mom	Younger brother
	Best friend, Michelle	Best friend, Michelle
	Older brother	Boyfriend, Phil
	Richard Nixon	Fiancé, Phil
1980s	Husband, Phil	Only daughter, Kate
	All disco musicians	Older son, Travis
	Ronald Reagan	Southerners
	Myself	Best friends, Holly & Nancy

1990s	Only daughter, Kate	Husband, Phil
	Older son, Travis	Younger son, Jack
	Professor York	Numerous best friends
	Oncologist	Oncologist
	Clinton/Tripp/Lewinsky/ Starr/Gingrich	Jimmy Carter

Becoming Santa to Santa

For me, the transition from receiving Santa to being Santa was a coming of age. It hadn't occurred to me that older Santas age and need younger Santas to carry on. My student Julie Selden wrote about having to become Santa after her father died:

> A few weeks before December 25, we kids start thinking about what to get Mom. We know she'll wake up with us on Christmas morning and there has to be *something* there. It's scary to know that it won't just appear; it's up to us.
>
> The first time we decided to buy her a CD player for

$55 from Huppin's Hi-Fi Phono and Video. The salesman in the store was nice to the three of us, all under the age of 18. We looked at all of the CD players. Jonathan wanted to buy the best and most expensive, but that was shot out of the water because he didn't have Mom's credit card to back him up. I wanted the sensible model, which was in our price range and was sleek and portable. Steven didn't care what we did. We put all of our $10 and $1 bills on the counter of the store, came up with exactly $55, and came home with a toy that Mom would never expect her teenage Santas to give.

On Christmas Eve we made Mom go up to her room with a promise that she wouldn't listen to us and would not come out to lay our gifts around the room until we told her to. The CD player was arranged with her stocking and an Anne Murray CD on the corner piece of the couch, and we draped a blanket over it. Then we went to bed and she came down and laid out our gifts. We didn't even leave cookies and milk out like we used to. We've come to an understanding. We're not orthodox Santas.

For some, the experience of becoming Santa is complicated. My friend Gordon Davis decided to play anonymous Santa to his parents one Christmas. He writes:

It was 1966 and my wife and I were living in New York, 2,000 miles from my parents in Idaho. It was a good year financially, and we felt grateful and generous. But as we thought of sharing our good fortune, we became aware that an act of sharing might create bad feelings. If we gave my parents a large, expensive gift, it might overshadow and detract from the gifts of the other children of the family. Se we decided, in the true spirit of Christmas, to give them a portable dishwasher anonymously and say it was from Santa Claus.

Dishwashers were a luxury item to my parents' generation. We had often heard them speak of a dishwasher as not being as good as hand washing, but we felt the comments were unconvincing. Also, the cost was high in terms of their financial situation. So we thought a dishwasher would be a great aid to them, even though their mental set was against purchasing one of their own, an ideal gift—something they would not get for themselves but would enjoy if they received it.

Being 2,000 miles away presented a problem in giving such a gift. Sending money and telling them to buy a dishwasher just didn't seem consistent with the idea of an anonymous Santa Claus. But, fortunately, we knew one of their good friends who was an engineer in the construction industry. He could get one for us and deliver it. We telephoned him and explained what we wanted. He was delighted at the idea of being part of the Christmas intrigue, and he agreed to handle the purchase and delivery of the dishwasher. He had the true spirit of anonymous Christmas giving. He was so anonymous that he didn't report back to us. Our only other contact with him was the invoice long after Christmas.

On Christmas morning, we made the customary holiday telephone call and talked with Mother and Dad about their Christmas. There was no mention of the dishwasher. I thought, "It didn't get delivered," and had a hard time not asking about it.

But, just as we were ready to say good-bye, Mother remarked, "I had a strange thing happen. I had a dishwasher delivered that belongs to someone else." I managed to evidence a slight interest, and then the story came out.

The gift was delivered on Christmas Eve. My father wasn't home when two delivery men came to the door and asked if it was the Davis residence. When Mother said it was, they brought in the dishwasher. Like true Christmas elves, they went straight to their work, unpacked the dishwasher, made the faucet adjustment, and left. Mother accepted the delivery because she assumed it was a gift from Dad. Even though she had reservations about its cost, she was excited and pleased with the gift.

When Dad came home, he denied all knowledge of the dishwasher. Having been married to him for over forty years, she knew he was telling the truth.

Mother had the horrible thought of some woman not receiving her Christmas gift because it had been mistakenly delivered to her. Her concern at another woman's disappointment spurred her into activity to locate the woman who was supposed to get the dishwasher. However, finding the real owner proved to be a problem. The two men had come in an unmarked pickup truck and had not been very talkative. In the brief casual conversation during unpacking, they had said that they worked out of Shelley, a small town ten miles away. She hadn't asked for more details. It didn't seem necessary at the time.

Mother immediately tried to redress the mistaken delivery. She called the appliance dealer in town, but he didn't know anything because it had come through a construction wholesaler. There was no dealer in the town of Shelley, where the men claimed to be from. She called the people with the same house number on the next street. She called the man down the block with the same last name. Had he purchased a dishwasher for his wife?

"Heck, no! I'm the best dishwasher there is." She called the dozen other Davises in the city, but no one had any knowledge of the misplaced gift.

Having failed in her search for the "rightful" owner, Mother resolved not to use the dishwasher and to wait for the dealer to retrieve it when the mistake was discovered. The new appliance stood in the kitchen with the instruction booklet and sample of dishwashing powder still inside to attest to its unused state.

As we listened on Christmas morning to the tale, the difficulties of giving anonymously were immediately apparent. But how could we get her to accept the gift without revealing we had sent it? I said as casually as I could, "Mother, it is obviously from Santa Claus." But that long-distance telephoned assurance didn't do the job.

Some action was required if the dishwasher was ever to see a dirty dish, so I called my brother, who lived in the same town, later in the day and told him that the dishwasher really was Mother's. Only after he solemnly assured her that he knew the giver and there was no mistake did she decide to use the dishwasher from the anonymous Santa Claus. Mother was never told who gave the gift to her.

When we visit my parents, the dishwasher sits in the kitchen and rekindles within us the excitement of getting Mother to accept a gift from Santa Claus.

I did not become Santa as early as Julie nor as oddly as Gordon. Nor did I anticipate how it would come about. When I went to Europe for three years in my early twenties, my grandmother, who had lived with my family since I was three, who baked fresh bread every week, who played a thousand games of Chinese Checkers and Muggins with me when my parents were out, defeating me without mercy and laughing as she did so, and who sat habitually by the piano when I practiced, her arm resting at the edge of the keys, was sending signals that I ignored. Then eighty-five, she implied she could live if I came home in two years, but not in three.

"Nonsense, Grandma," I said. "You'll be here when I get back. You'll live to be a hundred." Youthful babbling, pure and simple. In retrospect, I can see that I did not want to hear of it. When I left for the airport, she struggled out of her chair, gave me a hug with all the strength her shaking arms could muster, and stroked my cheek. She was crying. Needlessly, I thought.

I'd be back. She'd be here. "'Bye, Grandma," I said, and gave her a quick kiss. "I'll see you in three years."

On my second anniversary in Austria, at exactly eight o'clock in the morning, I retrieved two letters from the mailbox. One from my father said that Grandma was slipping away. It then ended, "Forget what I said. She just asked for an egg."

A second letter from my friend Russ Jensen had no such upbeat ending. "If you have anything to say to your grandmother, say it now."

My father's attempt to be reassuring didn't carry the credibility of Russ's letter. The thought struck me that I must call immediately. It was midnight at home. I'd have to wait a few hours. I biked to the post office, where, in 1962, you could place an international call that would go through in a few hours. I arranged to return for the call at 4:00 P.M., when it would be 6:00 A.M. at home. My father answered.

"Dad, how's Grandma?" I asked.

"Grandma died at midnight last night, Tom."

"She was crying for you when she died," my mother said. "She had us play the tape of the Vienna Choir Boys until the last moment." Her words fell like granite blocks.

The tape had been my gift to her at Christmas, just one month before. In an Austrian music store I had come upon a recording of the Vienna Choir Boys singing carols. Smitten with their high-pitched, lilting tones, which floated into the gothic arches of the Hofburg Chapel and drifted ever so gently down again like a silk scarf in a light breeze, I bought the tape and listened to it several times myself. The tones of the choir tendered the sounds of angels, not too close, not too distant, not present, but imminent. "Es ist ein Ros' entsprungen," and "O Du Fröhliche."

I would share my Austrian Christmas with my grandmother, I thought. And I would write her about roast goose for Christmas dinner with a Viennese family, about helping them light the Christmas-tree candles—real candles—for just a few moments while we sang "Stille Nacht, heilige Nacht." I would not tell her that in the midst of the charm of that Christmas, I still missed home.

Letters from my parents told me how Grandma listened to the recording again and again. When the tape ended, she would ask my mother to rewind it and start it over. I had overlooked—ignored—denied—the comments in their letters that Grandma had become weaker, bedridden. Then came the letters from Dad and Russ. A doctor friend has since told me that when someone says they are going to die at a certain time, you'd better pay attention. They are going to die, just at the moment they say it will happen. I left the post office stunned.

Unwittingly, unwillingly, I had become my grandmother's last Santa. A Santa, unfortunately, filled with denial. Not the Santa bringing life, but the Santa foreshadowing death. In the coming weeks and years I assembled and reassembled my vision of her dying, a dying that I missed, a chain of fragmented images leading to an end. I had called in the angels, as Horatio said, flights of angels singing her to her rest.

Dear Santa,

I have a rather unusual request. My husband, Paul, died two years ago, and Father's Day, anniversaries, and birthdays are still difficult. Christmas, however, is especially lonely. Paul used to say that during the year he had eight kids and a wife . . . but during the month of December he just had *nine* kids.

Lately I've been wondering what he is doing to fill his time while he waits for me. I'd like to make sure he has some of his favorite things this Christmas. First, how about a football and a jersey with a number 3 on it. Maybe he could start the HFL (Heavenly Football League) and play quarterback again. He'd have some great receivers.

The next thing would be lots of yellow legal pads and some black marker pens. These would be for the screenplays he never had a chance to write. You know he was working on the final draft of "Nicholas," a television special about you and the many legends of St. Nicholas. Maybe he could finish that.

Finally, I don't even know if fishing is allowed, but he loved deep-sea fishing. So a pole, tackle, and a Nep-Tuna reel would be great. I'm sure he would "catch and release."

If anyone can do this, Santa, I know you can. Milk and cookies will be in the regular place.

Mary Ellen, age 57

Dear Santa,

Instead of my usual list, I just want to thank you for Christmas Past. I can't remember the particulars of every single one, but my general recollection of all my Christmases is as warm and fuzzy as a chubby infant zipped into footed pajamas.

Remember that Christmas in Hawaii? Christmas Eve. Seven-year-old Jonathan, who still believed in you, was helping me set out some cookies and milk for you. He'd been looking forward to Christmas for weeks, talking about what he hoped you'd bring and how much fun he'd have Christmas morning tearing into the gifts, then playing with them all day long. When we had finished setting things up for your arrival, he dug out a crayon and a piece of notebook paper and announced he was going to leave a note for you. I left him to his work and went after the rest of the kids, chasing them to bed with the parents' perennial Christmas Eve threat: "Don't you know Santa can't come until all the kids are asleep?"

Hours after he and the rest of the kids were in bed and asleep, I slipped out to the living room to make sure the Christmas stage was set. Perched on a branch of our Christmas tree was his note, and being the nosy person that I am, I took it down and read it.

"Dear Santa," it said in his seven-year-old's scrawl. "Thanks for all the presents and all the good things you do. This is for you, to help a little for presents for other kids. Love, Jonathan." Tucked inside his note was Jonathan's life savings: a single dollar bill.

Sorry, Santa, but I kept the note. It was the best present I got that year.

You know, wonderful Christmas memories like this one, memories sandwiched between stories from Charles Dickens, Clement Moore, and St. Luke, have been the best presents I could have ever asked for.

Thank you for knowing what I really needed. And thanks for giving it to me.

Chris, age 44

Blue Christmas

We slogged slowly, ceremoniously toward the Christmas of 1997. It started well before Thanksgiving. Louise had an idea that seemed right. "Look," she said, fixing me in her unflinching gaze, "let's not have the Thanksgiving hassle this year. Let's not have everyone over here for the usual feast and torture ourselves fixing turkey, yams, and pies. The house is a mess for days afterwards, and then we face Christmas."

She had my attention. I recalled the last Thanksgiving. A crowded dining room, elbow to elbow. Grandchildren screaming. Dogs howling. Migraines. The house had started to empty out right after dinner because our married children had to go to their in-laws' for another dinner. Their children had screamed as they hauled them into the autumn air and buckled them into car seats for another hour of driving. Louise and I had sat in dismay when it was all over, staring at the fire.

"What do you have in mind?" I asked.

"Let's have Thanksgiving dinner this year on Wednesday night at the Lion House," she said. "Let them fix the meal, serve us, and clean up. They have gorgeous private dining rooms and great food; no one will have to eat two gigantic meals on the same day; and we can have some civility."

The next Sunday, when our sons and their families were visiting, she announced the plan. "Okay, listen up," she said. "Thanksgiving this year will be on Wednesday night in the Lion House. Wear your best clothes. No casual dress. Get babysitters. No children are invited."

First there was silence, then a few snorts from our sons. They hated dressing up. They hated formality. Their idea of a good dinner is throwing a couple of pizzas on a coffee table in front of a TV. "What are you saying?" someone wanted to know. It was a sincere question born of confusion. "Thanksgiving is a family time, and you're telling us to leave the children home?"

"Look," Louise countered. "We want to have Grandpa and Grandma Roos and Grandma Plummer there. Grandma

Plummer is ninety-four, and she and Grandma Roos don't like a lot of noise and confusion anymore. If we have only adults, we can have a pleasant dinner, you can talk to the grandparents, and we'll all have a nice time. Besides, you'll take your children to their other grandparents' on Thanksgiving Day. They'll have Thanksgiving dinner then, and they'll be a lot happier that they're not being hustled from one place to another. It's hard on them."

Louise prevailed. "And come on time," she said. "We don't want to hold up dinner for latecomers."

They came. On time. *Sans* children, confusion, barking dogs, and bloody noses. They came dressed up. There are pictures from that evening of the family eating turkey and pumpkin pie. Of brothers hugging brothers. Of wives hugging wives. Of everyone hugging grandparents. Of Ed kneeling beside Grandma Plummer. Even on his knees he's a head taller than she is, which always makes her giddy. And they show Louise's mother calm, relaxed, and smiling.

We would need the memories of that evening together. On December 18, less than a month later, just as I was thinking about Christmas and gifts and bills, my sister called from her home in Provo. "We've got a problem," she said. "I've been on the phone with Mom, and she just quit talking."

"I'll go right over," I said.

Mother was still living in the house she'd moved into more than sixty years earlier. She was still gardening. She could still remember funerals from sixty years ago. She had been "reading" books for the blind on tapes from the public library for more than a year. Her favorite, she told me, was the biography of Cary Grant. "I just love him," she said. I'd never heard my mother say anything like that about any other man than my father. Now, in her ninety-fifth year, she was divulging a passion for Cary Grant.

I broke into her house, which is just a few blocks from ours in Salt Lake City. And there I found her, slumped back on the bed, the phone still in her hand. Emergency crews came and went, expressing sympathy. I sat beside her body, alone and stunned.

Soon friends began to call. "What a blessing," they said. "I hope I die that fast." "She had a wonderful, full life." "She cared for herself to the very end."

Yes. All true. But I could not dismiss the death scene from my mind. I could not adjust to the first Christmas of my fifty-eight years without her. A thousand images passed again and again through my mind. Mother baking Christmas fruitcakes for friends and neighbors; Mother making timbales; Mother sitting on my lap when I played Santa Claus the first time; Mother lying back on the bed with the phone in her hand, her once-laughing expression contorted into death.

"Christmas is our busy season," a mortician told me as he chauffeured the family home from the cemetery. "And January is the second busiest time. Suicide month. We have to brace ourselves for that." His tone was so matter-of-fact, so businesslike. It was irrelevant. I was entrenched in gloom.

Nothing meant much to me that Christmas—not family gatherings, not gifts, not even the little kids talking about Santa Claus. I didn't do my usual Santa dress-up. I canceled a couple of visits I had promised to other families. I tried to muster a smile, an occasional laugh. The fact was, the words of the Preacher in Ecclesiastes made more sense: "Vanity of vanities; all is vanity."

With time, my feelings and memories became blurred and softened. When they thought I was ready, my children told their own stories about Grandma's passing, stories about the grandchildren that hadn't come out before, stories that might have seemed slightly off-key during the darkest time, but now had a healing power all their own.

Our granddaughter Rian's goldfish died shortly before Grandma Plummer. Its name was Jughead. That morning Rian had not yet noticed the fish floating on its side at the top of the bowl. Her parents were trying to keep it a secret by spelling the name of the fish when discussing its demise. But Rian, who was three, caught on to the spelling ruse. "Jughead?" she asked. "What happened to Jughead?"

"Jughead died," Dede said. "Do you want to help put him in the toilet?"

"Yes," Rian said.

So they scooped the fish out of the bowl with a cup and took it ceremoniously to the toilet. Rian put it in, and Dede flushed.

Rian jumped. "Why did you flush it?" she hollered. She had expected the fish to resume a happy life again in the toilet. Now suddenly it was gone.

"Well," Dede said, trying to keep a calm, parental voice, "Jughead is dead and he's gone to heaven."

"Is that where heaven is?" Rian yelled, pointing into the toilet.

For Rian, the death of her great-grandmother was like the death of her beloved Jughead. When her parents broke the news to her about Great-grandma, Rian pondered it for a moment and said, "Sometimes you have to flush old people too, huh?"

When my daughter-in-law Erica told her daughter Anne that Great-grandma Plummer had died, Anne wanted to know why.

"Because she got really old," Erica said.

"Well," Anne said, "we're not going to get old, because we don't drink alcohol."

Hearing these stories, I recalled a faint image from my own childhood. My Grandfather Plummer died when I was three. I was climbing the stairs to the mortuary with my cousin Patsy, who was ten days older than I. It must have been the evening of the viewing. The adults, I suspect, were as dumbfounded at Grandpa's sudden passing as I was at my mother's. He had died at our home while my mother was putting me down for a nap. "He lay down to rest. I was out of the room for three minutes," she often recounted, "and when I came back he was gone."

The dismay escaped my cousin and me. For us there was

no demarcation between life and death, no grief to be dealt with.

Patsy put it succinctly. "We're going to heaven," she said as we climbed up the stairway.

From my adult perspective, I wonder how the experience of children can be so different. Theirs is so fresh and full of life. Maybe that's why we needed to get away from them at least for Thanksgiving dinner. It was just too much freshness, too much energy. We needed time to be older together.

But I needed the children to breathe new life into a time of grieving. It was a cyclical thing. First I needed time with adults. Then I needed time with children to bring me back around. Santa needs the children as much as the children need Santa. "Children are the keys of Paradise," R. H. Stoddard once wrote. Maybe he meant that children see things more deeply than the adults around them, whose minds have been imprisoned by age and reason. In the face of death they are a source of humor, goodwill, and life. Whittier may have gotten it just right:

God hath his small interpreters;
The child must teach the man.

Still, in retrospect, it was right last year for the adults to have their time together, and for the children to be spared. Why should they be subjected to the weightiness of adults who can no longer move so quickly, think so fast, or jump so high? They didn't need us at Thanksgiving dinner any more than we needed them. We needed them later, in the wake of that blue Christmas, when one Santa was dead and the others were grieving and could not help themselves so well. That was the time for a new spring, a new look at the world, and a climb up the stairs to heaven.

Dear Santa,

I'm the kid who asked you for a horse every year even though I lived in suburban Southern California then and had no place to keep it. (By the way, the Breyer horses were a nice gesture, one my parents must have appreciated, but model horses are a poor substitute for the real thing. My imagination could ride them only so far. I go much farther now on my real horse Ben, but I must admit that the Breyers are still my favorite mounts for riding off into my childhood.) Also I've left you a piece of my birthday cake with a tall glass of milk and a thank-you note every Christmas Eve since about 1955. In fact, I actually believed that you, not the proverbial stork, had delivered me to my parents, along with all their other Christmas presents, until I was in third grade when Bobby, the sleazy kid next door, finally convinced me that sex, not Santa, was responsible for human reproduction—even though he was rather hazy about the biological details.

Oh, and my kids always display their Santa gifts from the year before right beside their Christmas stockings to demonstrate to you how well they've taken care of them. (By the way, Travis still feels bad about losing the C3PO chair litter to his Ewok Village within the first six months he had it. He thinks it may turn up yet, probably when he moves to college next year, and appreciates your not having held it against him.)

And you must remember my wife, Lu Ann. She's the one who puts her extensive collection of Santa figures (81 and counting) on prominent display throughout the house during the holidays (not that any representation, however artistically rendered, could do justice to your actual presence, of course). She was born on New Year's Eve (exactly a week after I was) but never once thought she might have been delivered to her parents by Baby New Year (who probably has enough trouble just delivering himself—or herself—it's hard to distinguish gender in a baby wearing a diaper and banner). Lu Ann keeps the Christmas spirit better than anyone I know (and she's also pretty clear on the biological details, if you get my drift).

If you still can't remember me, just have one of the elves look me up on your database.

Anyway, I'm writing to ask for an extra portion of Christmas spirit for my family this year. Since Lu Ann's cancer diagnosis this spring, we've all had the feeling that we need to treasure up our experiences together a little more intently than we have before. We've already enjoyed many wonderful Christmases together in the past, as you probably know, but this year we'd appreciate an extra magical Christmas to enjoy in the present. Next year we'll deal with our hopes for Christmas future. In the meantime, enjoy your usual slice of my birthday cake. (It'll be red and white Waldorf Astoria cake, but we've switched to nonfat milk, so be forewarned.)

Finally, I'll just say, thank you, Santa, for everything.

Your friend,
Phillip, age 45

Dear Santa,

That loaded bag of yours
Has produced the most amazing things—
A Toni doll with real hair to style
Tinker toys, a shiny scooter to ride freestyle
A red taffeta dress, nurses' kits
Nancy Drew mysteries for shivering fits
Long blue skis for racing down hills
A record player for rock and roll thrills . . .
You've brought such smiles in the past
I'd like to thank you and your all-star cast.
It seems impossible—such happiness just for the asking
How lucky can one get?
But this year is different,
I'm afraid to admit.
My wish is of a different kind,
One I doubt you'll be able to find
In that big bag . . .
But I'll ask anyway, with a prayer
Is there a cancer cure somewhere in there?

                    Hopefully,
                    Suzanne, age 57

The "Truth" about Santa Claus

Our five-year-old granddaughter Anne popped a question on her mom recently that caught her off guard: "Mom, does Santa Claus have claws?" This is the same child who put a tough question to me last summer when she and her three-year-old brother, Harrison, were visiting:

It was August. Geraniums, roses, and petunias were out. Leaves and grass were green, skies were blue, temperatures in the nineties. Nothing had signaled the arrival of fall; there had been no indication that winter and Christmas would ever come. Not even the malls had put up plastic trees and Santa-land booths to herald the onset of the money season.

We were walking around the block, sipping Slurpees, when Anne asked, "Grandpa, does Santa really go down chimneys?"

Before I could answer, Harrison chimed in, "Yeah, Tom, how's he do that?"

I looked at the houses around me. They all had chimneys. Had she noticed them and wondered how a fat man would get through? Or wondered how Santa would get in her chimney-less apartment? Or was this the tip of a deeper question, like, does Santa really exist? A memory of her father's own chimney art, a plate he made when he was in fifth grade, came to mind:

I went for the quick way out. "Well, I guess he's just magic," I said.

"He's not magic," Anne shot back.

I tried to keep my mouth from breaking into a smile. "If he isn't magic," I said, "how does he get his reindeer to fly?"

"The reindeer are magic," she said without a second's hesitation. "But not Santa Claus."

It seemed like a signal, a sign of the transition, however early, of her emergence into the rational world, that sad metamorphosis when the boundaries between fantasy and mundane reality are no longer fluid. Certainly her question was different from Harrison's. He was still wondering not "if" but "how." Anne's question was "does he really."

I suppose every adult who spends time with children has to deal with the question. Some parents simply oppose the whole idea of Santa. My student Dianna Douglas wrote, "I've never believed in Santa Claus, because it is silly. None of my family has—we just talk about him like a fun myth, apparently because Mom went through an identity crisis when she stopped believing. She stopped believing in God and didn't trust her parents for months."

Although she reported no such familial trauma, Marie

Nelson agreed with Dianna: "I never believed in Santa Claus. My mother is strongly opposed to the whole idea. Santa Claus just takes away from the real meaning of Christmas, which is Christ. It is confusing to little children to teach that the reason we celebrate Christmas is because of Jesus and then have pictures of Santa around."

Some people, on the other hand, advocate his reality with a great fervor. A man by the name of Frank Church wrote in the September 21, 1897, edition of the *New York Sun*, "Not believe in Santa Claus! You might as well not believe in fairies. . . . Nobody sees Santa Claus, but that is no sign there is no Santa Claus. The most real things in the world are those which neither children nor men can see. No Santa Claus! Thank God! he lives and he lives forever."

Maybe some grandchild had just pinned Mr. Church to the wall. Maybe he had felt ambushed by her forthright inquisition and used his job with the newspaper to defend himself and all other parents caught in the same web. If I'd thrown that argument at my kids when Louise was listening, she would've said, "Oh, give me a break."

Discovering that Santa Claus is not what you thought he was is, to be sure, traumatic for some folks. My mother remembered to the last day of her life how she discovered Santa. As a child she lived in Monroe, a small town in southern Utah. At Christmastime everyone would gather at the Old South Church for a big community dinner. These were stone-broke farmers whose big Christmas present for the children was an orange and a few nuts—food they could only afford or even find just once a year. They would put on their best clothes—coarse, heavy, woolen fabrics that were turned into quilts when they were no longer suitable as clothing—and celebrate the season together.

The great event of the evening was the arrival of Santa Claus, whose very presence attested to well-being in spite of their hard lives. When Santa Claus, with his abundance of candy and presents, appeared at the Old South Church, the day-to-day work of tending farms, milking cows, and dragging wood for stoves out of the surrounding hills melted away. Santa gave respite and a little relief from the harsh world outside.

I inferred from my mother's accounts of those Christmas festivals that to the children, who worked nearly as hard as the adults, Santa Claus proffered hope for a better life.

And so it was in the joy of this occasion that my mother

attended the Christmas dinner in her seventh or eighth year. The meal was lavish, and people ate more than they had since last Christmas—ham or turkey or beef under great piles of mashed potatoes from the fall harvest. For dessert there were homemade pies with ice cream turned from the heart-stopping rich milk of the local Jersey cows. And when all were filled with food and anticipation, Santa arrived.

"Oh, it was thrilling," my mother would say in her retelling. She'd look upward and spread her fingers outward on both hands, as she must have done when she was an excited little girl on Christmas Eve, 1910. "He'd come prancing into the hall of the church and we'd sit on his lap and he'd give us candy. We didn't have candy except at Christmas, you know." She'd pause to relish once again that long-past scene when all was right with the world.

But this one time, this terrible night, everyone was so excited that Santa just couldn't control himself. He got up and did a little dance. My mother's autobiography relates the occasion: "He got by with the masquerade until he began to tap dance, and my heart dropped down to my shoes. He wasn't Santa, he was Grandpa."

"Nobody in town could dance like that," she told me

eighty-five years after the event. "Only Grandpa Warnock. There he was in his red suit and hat and dancing Grandpa's jig. I felt just sick. I was so upset I went home and cried."

I have seen pictures of Great-grandpa Warnock. He had a beard. He looked Santa-Claus-ish, except that he was too thin for our modern, robust images of the old fellow. "Was that the first time you recognized him?" I would ask—this story had become ritual between us.

"Oh, yes," she'd say. "I had no idea."

"Did he wear a fake beard? How did he disguise himself?"

"No, he had his own beard," she'd say. "He didn't need another beard. He just wore a Santa suit."

I could never figure out how Great-grandpa Warnock could just put on a Santa suit, keep his own beard and hair, and not be recognized; how my mother knew he was a fake only when he began to dance. Surely she would know it was her grandfather with a red suit on?

But I wasn't any more insightful. I believed in Santa Claus until I was nine. For years I was embarrassed that it took so long until a friend recently told me he was twelve. I think most of my friends were believers too. If they weren't, they never told me.

My discovery happened on the Christmas when I asked Santa for ice skates. My mother brought home skates a couple of weeks before Christmas, saying she had to find out what size I wore so she could let Santa know. These were not the skates I would get, she said, just a trial pair. I put them on and skated around the living room carpet. She took them back, and that was that. Santa would deliver them on Christmas Eve.

A week or so before Christmas, I was rummaging through a closet looking for something and, lo and behold, there were the skates. I backed out of the closet in disbelief, trying to assimilate what I had just learned, scrambling to reorganize the world as I knew it.

That night I went to my mother, who was standing at the stove stirring a pot of wassail. "Mom," I said. "Is there really a Santa Claus?"

She looked a little startled, continued to stir, and remained quiet.

"Mom," I said. "I want to know. Is there a Santa Claus?"

She looked me straight in the eye and said, "He's the spirit of Christmas."

"But is there a Santa Claus? Is he real?"

"He's the spirit of Christmas," she repeated.

To this day I remember a surge of irritation shooting up my spine. I wanted the hard facts, and she was giving me abstractions. I tried again, dancing on one foot and then the other. "Is there a Santa Claus?"

"It's the spirit of Christmas." And that's all she would say. I got not one more syllable out of her on the subject.

Looking back, I think it was a pretty good answer, an answer I now realize that many parents give. She might have set me down and delivered a sermon on the real spirit of Christmas, the birth of Jesus, the religious depth and breadth of the occasion, which I already knew as a nine-year-old boy. Then she might have launched into an explanation of the medieval, historical origins of Santa Claus via St. Nicholas and various ancient myths from the Greeks and the Egyptians. But she spared me. She left him enthroned where he's been for a long time—the elf who is the spirit of Christmas. The elf of yearning. The elf of hope. The elf of charity. Charity by grace, pure grace.

Phil Snyder's mother wouldn't answer him directly either. "As long as you believe in him, he will come," she said.

Some of my students have come to terms with Santa's

reality with a maturity that surprises me because I was just never that sophisticated. Matthew Harward writes:

> There was a Christmas in Bellevue that I remember. On Christmas Eve we watched an animated version of Dickens's *Christmas Carol*, drank hot apple cider, and ate homemade deep-fried doughnuts rolled in cinnamon, under the pervading smell of spruce from the tree in the corner that I would lie under at night with the lights on, the other lights off, and feel the frost form on the window. That night I slept upstairs with my older brother Neil. His room was in the corner, and the ceiling slanted. Late into the night we talked, a kind of talk that would make a six-year-old feel old and important when in a conversation with a sixteen-year-old brother, in his life so distant from mine.
>
> At some point I heard motion downstairs. Coming out of the depth of the midnight talk, I said, "I'll bet Santa's here."
>
> My brother rolled over onto his side, facing the wall. "Do you still seriously believe in Santa Claus?" he asked, and the way with which he said it made me feel naive for carrying around such a belief. And that was it—my faith

in Santa Claus, with no proof, no substantiation, seen or otherwise, was gone. I barely even felt it go.

And so I knew that the sounds I heard were from my parents, a revelation that didn't sadden me, only made them seem more important. "I wish there was a hole right here, so I could look down and see them," I said.

Shannon Murdock answered the question for herself during an argument in grade school. She writes:

In the second grade over red and white and green-sprinkled cookies, the girl across from me said to my friend, "You're stupid if you think Santa is real. It's just your parents. They're the ones who give you the presents."

My friend was looking worried, so I said, "No, sir. He's real."

"Nu-uh."

"Uh-huh."

"Nu-uh."

And then I had a solution: "Whether he's a man from the North Pole, or both of your parents sneaking around, he's still real."

Most of us eventually live with the paradox about the same way, if not with the same insight. When I see adults standing around in the mall watching their little ones sitting on Santa's knee, they don't look skeptical. They instinctively become the children on his lap. He's as real as real can be.

He's just as real to people whose children have grown up and left home. A few years ago on Christmas Eve our friend Francine Bennion was grieving to her husband, Bob, that Santa Claus had left their home and lives for good. Their children had moved away for professions and families of their own. Yes, an adult daughter and a friend were visiting them for Christmas, but it was not the same. Their Christmas tree, decorated in the family traditions, had only the packages Bob and Francine had wrapped for each other and their guests beneath it, making their celebration of the holiday seem all too sparse. Santa Claus was missing, and Francine was sad.

"Santa will never visit our home again," she said to Bob.

And just at that moment—this is the absolute truth—just at that moment, I stood at their door in my Santa suit and rang the bell, a dorky neighbor via *santa ex machina* bringing chocolate kisses to a few people he loved. But what Francine saw was not a dork. What Francine saw through the window that bleak Christmas Eve was the real Santa Claus, the one she had just proclaimed gone from her life.

As I think back on the moment, everything goes into slow motion. I see Francine coming along the hallway, looking out, grinning broadly. She reaches for the latch, swings the door open wide. "It's Santa Claus. Bob, come here, it's Santa Claus." She turns back to me and says, "I just told Bob we would never have another visit from Santa Claus, and here you are. You're here."

"Yup, I'm here," I said. "But I'm a little surprised you doubted me, Francine."

She gave me a big Christmas hug. "I should not have doubted you."

"You should never doubt Santa Claus, Francine," I said.

The fact is, Santa stays with us. He spans our transitions from childhood to adulthood. He symbolizes the kindly adult male that men wish they could be and women keep hoping to find, if even under a rock. He symbolizes joy and freedom, the flow between fantasy and reality that is all too often lost as we cross into our adult years. And who is to say that the modern world of blaring horns, cartwheeling stock markets, and nuclear threats from developing countries is more real than the world of Santa Claus, where dreams are realized and goodness, kindness, and pure love prevail?

The more the world becomes enmeshed in its own traps, the more it grinds even its inventors to bits in its unstoppable gears, the more it rushes to create a computer named "Hal" to take over the decisions of mere mortals, the closer it comes to creating human clones and then armies of clones, the more the world of Santa Claus calls to me, the more its joys and freedoms speak to me.

Does Santa really exist? Does he really hook up reindeer and spread gifts through the world in a single night? No. But it's a true story. It's a true story of the human capacity for love, generosity, and mercy. It's a true story about how readily accessible his workshop is to people of goodwill, of all ages. It's a true story of our own lives as we struggle to reconcile the world of dreams and fantasies and possibilities with the so-called real world. One of my students wrote that although her parents never took her to malls or tried to push the literal idea of Santa, "They taught me to believe in the spirit of Santa Claus, the loving, giving, Christmas feeling. Then if I had ever believed in Santa Claus—the actual person—and stopped, I would still have something to believe in."

In the end, just when we think we have it all figured out, it's the children who leave us with no easy answers, just hard questions. A friend told me a story recently. She sat beside her small grandson Christopher, who lay dying of a neuroblastoma in an oncology unit for children at UCLA hospital. It was an unreal place in a real world, she said. Bald children everywhere. Clowns came to visit and entertain. Jugglers. Balloon artists. A kindly death camp, but a death camp nonetheless.

Christopher had survived Christmas, but the chill January air marked his turn to die. He lay on his hospital bed with family gathered around, family grieving for the death of one so young, family exhausted and distraught from months of hospital stays and rising and falling hopes. Family pleading with God to save the life of this child. They could not keep him. He was leaving. Then came a moment that my friend said got her through the whole ordeal. Shortly before the last breath came, little Christopher looked up at the ceiling as if it had opened into the sky above, smiled, and said, "Look—it's Santa Claus."